BOSS UP!

A
GUIDE TO
CONQUERING
AND LIVING
YOUR
BEST LIFE

CHIKA IKE

Boss UP!:
A Guide to Conquering and Living Your Best Life
Copyright © 2018 by Chika Ike

ISBN: 978-1-54393-073-3
eBook ISBN: 978-1-54393-074-0

CHIKA IKE IS A FAMOUS NIGERIAN ACTRESS WHO has had leading roles in over a hundred movies. She conceived, produces, and presents the popular TV series *African Diva Reality Show*.

She is an entrepreneur who owns a fashion brand and is also a real estate developer. She set up a foundation that helps underprivileged children access an education, and she has studied for a PLD at Harvard. Now she has written a book.

Boss UP! helps you climb the ladder, step across any missing rungs, and never look down, just as she did.

In loving memory of my

father and mother,

with thanks for giving my life

a purpose and meaning;

And to my

five brothers and sisters,

with thanks for always being

my greatest cheerleaders.

Do it
TIRED
Do it
SCARED
Do it
CONFUSED
Just
DO IT!

Chika Ike

CONTENTS

Part 3 BUSINESS

Part 4 SOCIETY

Part 5 FAMILY AND RELATIONSHIPS

Part 6 GRACE

Introduction

'Life is a matter of choices, and every
choice you make makes you.'

John C. Maxwell

Good to meet you. If you're ambitious, this book's for you.

I'm happy now, but I wasn't always. A lot of young people
have waded into careers and relationships as confused and
doubtful as I was. I made a few good moves early on, but
I also made many of the classic, eye-rolling, self-defeating mistakes. By Bossing Up and changing my attitude, I
changed my life. I chose to be happy, successful, ambitious,
and driven, and you can too.

This book will show you how to work around the obstacles and get your life moving smoothly the first time. I explain how I failed, how other people failed me, and how I sometimes, somehow, got it right. I hope that by sharing my mistakes, you won't have to make them. Mistakes such as... allowing relationships to define me, hiding away because I hated my looks, wondering whether all the hard work was worth the effort, being bullied because I was different, and more. I wish I'd had this book to read when I was younger.

The 41 chapters in *Boss UP!* cover most of the obstacles we all confront—fear, convention, love, money, self-esteem. Some are internal, existing only in our minds, and some are external, found in other people's attitudes. Part 1, titled 'Chikadibia,' (which is my full name), explains my starting point and introduces the rest of the book in more detail.

Please dip in with both feet, and feel good. I hope your outcome is greater health, wealth, and happiness. And may your God be with you.

Chika

'Life is a
matter of
choices, and
every choice
you make
makes you.'

John C. Maxwell

PART 1

CHIKADIBIA

'Life is tough, my darling, but so are you.'

—Stephanie Bennett Henry

1

AN EARLY CRISIS

'You don't have to be great to start,
but you have to start to be great.'

Joe Sabah

I KEEP A VISION BOOK IN WHICH I NOTE MY current goals and dreams. You can start one on any day, in any month, but January is when we're all looking forward to a new start and it's when I set out my boldest aims for the year ahead. In 2010, 'Write a book' was on the top of my list. A brilliant idea. So brilliant that it sat at the top of the list every January until 2017—I still hadn't finished writing my book.

This year, 2018, 'Publish my book' is at the top of the list. Did I just procrastinate for seven years? No. Sometimes a goal is out of reach because we're not ready. We haven't yet done enough work, or had the right experience, or drawn coherent conclusions. Now I'm good to go. And I hope this book saves the reader some of the time that I spent finding out how to do what I've done.

I'm sitting on my bed in pyjamas, laptop on my knees, listening to a meditation song, which helps me concentrate. I have typed and deleted several times. I desperately want to start in a beautiful way and be as honest as I can be. I look around my room and feel grateful. I didn't grow up in such luxury. Life has thrown me plenty of curveballs. I have faced rejection and unkindness and manipulative people, but those difficulties have made me stronger. We must take what life offers us, and run with it.

Life offered me Papa Ajao, Mushin. Mushin is booming now, but our part of it was overcrowded then. We were a typical family: father, mother, six children in a three-bedroom flat in a block of six. The block needed repainting, and its gate hung of the hinges, but that didn't matter because we had a big compound with lots of kids my age to play with. On Saturdays we had a football match. I was no good at it, but when they finally made me goalkeeper, nothing got past me. I was in the goal every week from then on. We played hide and seek, and danced in the rain, and I would re-enact characters from Bollywood movies. Dad rented those from the video store on his way home from work. He never liked us playing in the compound, so when we saw his car in the distance we'd all race for the door and scamper up to our flat on the second floor.

My father was sometimes kind, but always strict. He didn't talk a lot. He was the baker who supplied the whole neighbourhood. Bread was one thing we never ran out of, and our visitors never went away without some fresh baked goods. I am kind of breaded-out as a result. I hardly ever eat it today, no matter how good it is.

My mum was very beautiful, always smiling and pleasant. She dressed all of us in our Sunday best when we went to church. Other children admired our outfits, and their mothers always said how respectful we were. If a grown-up offered us a coin as a present, we were taught never to accept it. If we did, Mum would smile indulgently for the benefit of the giver, but when we got home she'd spank us. And she'd do that even if she'd urged us, with the generous benefactor looking on, to take the money. So I, for one, would never ever take anything. All the same, she was a loving mother, and we all thought she was the best mum ever.

The bakery was booming, and my mum worked there too. We had two nannies. They used to chase us around the compound in the evenings before our baths, and in the mornings they'd get us out of bed despite every kind of resistance. We must have been a worrying and often annoying handful, but they loved us regardless. We wanted for nothing, and we learned to expect regular small pleasures. On Sundays we bought snacks in a fast-food restaurant after church, and headed home for Sunday rice. At Christmas we had new dresses, Christmas gifts, and as much chicken as we wanted.

Crisis? What crisis?

When I was eleven, my father's business collapsed. He couldn't pay the rent on our flat, and we had to move to his bakery. This meant occupying seven rooms in a half-built building surrounded by thick forest and sluggish canals full of snakes. It lacked key elements such as roofing, plaster on the walls, and toilet fittings. We'd look up and see intricate golden honeycombs, swarming with bees, suspended from the ceiling. Mosquitos floated constantly in and out of our new home, and great fluttering crowds of bats emerged at dusk to play hide and seek. The first morning after the move, I woke up covered in big itchy lumps, the mosquitos having feasted on my blood overnight.

It was better than living on the streets. We had enough to eat, although from then on we saw chicken only on high days and holy days, and our diet became mainly vegetarian. Beans featured in stews, and stews featured big-time. Our old school had been private and fee-paying, but now it was too expensive and too far away. The new one was almost free, and on the next street. I hated it, but of course, nothing could be done about that. Dad was already frustrated about his business. Mummy was the one who patiently listened to our complaints, dabbed cold pink calamine lotion onto our mosquito bites, and sprayed insecticide in all the rooms when we were at school. Sadly the nannies had to leave; but one of them, Rebecca, insisted on staying to help our mum for a year. Rebecca loved us so much. She was part of the family. I was very fond of her and always helped her in the kitchen. She nicknamed me Fancy Nancy. Fancy because I loved fashion and makeup and was always entertaining her with drama; Nancy, because it's my middle name.

My mother started catering for events, to support my dad and make ends meet. She also supplied doughnuts to our new school every morning before break-time. The principal used to entrust me with each day's payment to give to her in the afternoon. My mum and I had a special bond. It was a tough time for her, but she always wore a smile and told me, 'Tough times never last, but tough people do'.

I remembered that. God works in mysterious ways.

'You don't have to be great to start, but you have to start to be great.'

Joe Sabah

2

FACING REJECTION

Trying to Boss Up
(but not quite getting it, yet...)

POOR OR NOT, MY FAMILY HAD STATUS IN OUR community. We weren't rich, but we'd been better off, which gave my parents some standing. Mostly this was a case of the one-eyed leading the blind, although my mother came from a well-educated family and eventually she became a pastor. She had always gone out of her way to help anyone in need.

For me, growing up was tough with a dad like mine. I was only about six years old when I knew for sure that he didn't like me much. He blamed me for everything. Whenever I asked for something, he'd say no; but I'd see my older sister ask for the same thing, and he'd just give it to her. As we became older schoolgirls and had to ask for money—same story. And if there was an unpleasant task to be done, I was the one he ordered to do it.

Maybe you're reading this and thinking, *Oh, she must have been imagining it. Kids always feel aggrieved! Sibling rivalry is as old as time. Maybe she'd read* Cinderella *once too often? You know, a put-upon young girl whose ugly stepsisters go to the ball while she's supposed to stay home and scrub floors on her hands and knees.* But I didn't have any stepsisters. I was the fourth child in a family of six, and none of us was ugly. Our father was kind and generous to the others. Maybe it had something to do with who I was. Maybe I was a stepchild. I didn't really know what that meant, but I knew it would make me an outsider, a reason to be treated poorly.

One day I summoned up the courage to ask.

'Mommy, am I like the others? Am I yours and Daddy's?'

'Goodness, Chika, who else's would you be? What do you ask that for?'

'Daddy is always picking on me.'

'No, he isn't. Sometimes he just has other things on his mind. He has worries.'

But my brothers and sisters noticed too. None of us knew why he didn't like me. It couldn't be because I was a girl; he was fine with my sisters. In primary school if I needed money for books, he'd say a flat no and turn away. The others just asked and were given what they needed, with no argument. I'd have to ask my mother.

So I wasn't a stepchild, but I felt deeply that something was wrong with me—that I didn't fit into the family as the others did—and my parents wouldn't say what it was.

As we all grew up, we had a family picture taken every Christmas, with everybody dressed up and smiling. One time my mother placed me next to my father, and he visibly flinched. Sharply he told me to go to the end of the line, the edge of the picture.

When the photograph arrived, my mother saw it and frowned. I had my eyes all scrunched up and my face was shiny with tears. 'You look as if you're crying your eyes out. Was something the matter?'

'Daddy told me to stand away from him. Why doesn't he like me?'

'That's not true. Don't you ever think that.'

But she looked angry, and I heard them arguing afterwards. She was saying,

'After all these years, will you not let this thing go? It is affecting the child. She doesn't know why you are doing it, and she is hearing so many negative things from you.'

I didn't hear his response. What was 'this thing' that my mother mentioned? 'his thing' that my father wouldn't let go of?

When I had my first period, I didn't know quite what was going on or what to do about it. I stayed in my room. I didn't dare tell my mother in case she told Daddy and he got angry with me, so I hid in the wardrobe and hoped it would stop. After a while my sister came looking for me. She pulled me out, and I told her why I was hiding.

'No, of course he won't get angry with you. You will get a present!'

So I went to my mother, and she told me how to deal with periods and provided me sanitary protection. I didn't get a present, but she gave me my first sex education lesson then and there. I must at all costs stay away from boys, because if I sat in a boy's lap, I would get pregnant and if he hugged me, I'd have twins. (It's been a huge help in life to know this.)

After that, when I needed more protection and my mother was away, I could never get Daddy to give me the money, so I had to ask my older sister to ask him so that she could give it to me. But we fell out pretty often, the two of us, and once or twice she refused to ask, and we had to make up. If you are a girl reading this, you know that in X number of days you are going to need Tampax or whatever you use, and the days are always ticking down, and you don't want to feel mortified or ashamed to be without protection when your period starts. I was in and out of a mild anxiety all the time.

Later, when my mother was away doing her master's degree, I was a teenager and my siblings and I would sometimes sit in front of the TV watching *The Rich Also Cry.* We were crazy about it. Daddy always seemed to get irritated that I was there with the others. He'd order me into the kitchen to cook for him.

One day he asked my older sister to make him some food. She's no cook, and she said no. (I'd never have dared.) I was tired, I had been working all day, but he asked me to do it instead. So I started to cook, but found there wasn't any kerosene. I didn't know where my father was, so I snuck off to bed and fell asleep. At about eleven that night I woke up with a scream. Daddy was flogging me on the legs and bum with a belt.

'Next time when I tell you to cook, you COOK!'

'here's no kerosene!'

'DO it! Use firewood!' He whacked me again. My legs hurt, but I got up and did it.

I was too badly bruised to move the next day. My mother was back then, and she got really cross. She said to me she was sorry. She made excuses for him to me, but I don't think she held back when she talked to him. He was less objectionable for a while after that, but nothing really changed.

One day my sister and I had a serious fight, and she turned to me and said, 'I hate you. I see why Daddy doesn't like you.'

That hurt. But I knew it was true. I'd tried hard, but I just didn't know how to make him change. When I was accepted into the University of Lagos to study for a diploma (and later for a degree), he wouldn't pay the fees. I was making some money of my own by then, but not enough.

And then I got married.

3

LESSON (ALMOST) LEARNED

Learning to Boss Up Emotionally,
Socially, and Financially

I WAS NINETEEN WHEN I GOT ENGAGED. I HAD
been earning my own money for a while. But money is just one
empowering thing. The other, with far more potential for empowering a person, is love.

If you have a life partner who cares for you, someone who loves
you as much as you love them, you can do anything. I knew this. My
father may have had a blind spot where I was concerned, but he was
a good husband to my mum. He loved and respected my mother, and
she felt the same about him. They supported one another. Except for
his unreasonable attitude toward me, she supported him in everything. He was proud of her when she got a master's in theology and
became a renowned pastor.

So I had a clear idea of what a good marriage looked like when
I met my husband. I was already a model and actress. If I'd ever been

Cinderella, this man would have been (in my eyes) Prince Charming. He wasn't the kind of hunk you might imagine, but he seemed infatuated with me, and I was infatuated right back, and dropped my guard. I confided all my insecurities to him. I had started a movie career, and I was out in the world, making a name for myself, but I was still insecure about my inexperience, and the only person who really knew this was my husband-to-be. His work had nothing to do with the entertainment industry. He was successful in his steady, nine-to-ive job, and he had good promotion prospects.

Actors have to live with rejection as a routine. I hadn't quite worked that out yet. It didn't happen often, but when it did, I was upset. So I knew I needed a strong partner, and I thought I'd found one. I would be a young married woman, working and going to university. Eventually we would have children, but I wanted to have a career first, and travel.

I can't remember how much discussion my fiancé and I had about my sun-drenched vision of marriage and his ideas of a perfect life. Probably none.

I was so needy, so very much looking for devotion from a man. Love is blind. It finds what it wants to, and I decided he was The One. I trusted him. I thought he was an angel; he was so considerate of me. My guard was down. I told him all my weaknesses. I presented myself like a victim, and guess what? I was victimized.

The wedding was a few months away when he first became verbally controlling. If only I'd known that controlling behaviour was a symptom of a larger disease, like the first bumps before a full-blown case of measles, I'd have been able to stick up for myself. But I was just puzzled. All I knew was that I had to do things the way he wanted them done. ('Fetch!' I was being trained, like a pet dog.) Almost everything I did was wrong, and annoyed him, so I became meek and obedient. And I was sure I could change him, in time.

The day before the wedding, he hit me and walked out. I was shocked. An immediate flash of self-preservation, an instinct, told me to get a grip. Call off the wedding. Change the locks! But I was weakened by fear. I told myself it had been my fault. I must have seemed so annoying and stupid. I had deserved it. I would never say or do such things again.

And I couldn't stop now—the huge party, the guests, the spectacle, the fabulous clothes, the music, the laughter, the dancing, the food, the tributes. My parents' embarrassment and the gossip and ridicule. No, I couldn't call it off.

I had been shown a STOP sign—in neon letters twenty feet high—which should have made me come to a screaming halt. But I drove right through it. I was in love. When I looked at him, I saw a mirage of a strong man who would look after me. That person wasn't really there, but in my fantasy that's who he would become. So when he came back and cried and apologized and we hugged and kissed… I was convinced he'd never hit me again.

I was insecure. I hadn't yet learned independence of mind.

Do you know the story of Beauty and the Beast? It's a fairy tale, in which a beautiful princess falls deeply in love with a bad-tempered, hairy monster with honking breath. On their wedding day, he turns into a prince. Yes, girls… it's a story. I repeat: a story.

For me, marriage was constant humiliation. He cheated on me with other women. He found joy in hitting me; it made him feel better. Sometimes I suspected that he was jealous, because while I was doing well, he remained pretty much a drone. On the rare occasions when I dared to think like that, I also dared to think of divorcing him. But how could I? My mother was a pastor. She'd never be able to hold her head high again. The gossip… I could imagine the other mothers in the congregation. Scandal! The pastor's daughter—the one who's an actress—wants to leave her husband. It would be the sensation of the church.

I rationalized my fear of change. So I took the beatings. Not just because of my mother. I was scared of being humiliated too. If my marriage drifted onto rocks in front of the public, I'd look a fool. I was a celebrity, and if you think actresses aren't role models you're wrong. How could I destroy my carefully constructed illusion of a perfect life?

With the slightest provocation, he'd hit me. (I have to stick with this marriage, I thought. It will improve.) I tried martyrdom; I found a bottle of vodka he'd brought home, and drank myself into a stupor, knowing he'd be sorry.

What was I thinking? Self-harm, so that a bully will work out how much he loves me? When did that ever work?

A beaten wife is what they call co-dependent; that is, emotionally, and usually financially and socially, dependent on changing nothing. By putting up with the beatings, a co-dependent wife is collaborating with her husband. She's mutely telling him that he can get away with this. He can be as cruel as he likes for as long as he likes, and she'll still be there. It's the same if your man is a gambler or an alcoholic. The rule is: LEAVE. Leave now. Leave before the door slams behind you. If you have children, that door will stay slammed for a long time.

I'll tell you, later in this book, how I came to divorce him.

After the divorce, I understood why I'd married the wrong man. I talked to a therapist, who asked the right questions, and I came up with the answers for myself, the answers which—if I hadn't felt so low, so frightened, for so many years—I would have arrived at a lot sooner.

Firstly: I'd married that man because I wanted to show how grown up I was. And without even knowing it, I'd convinced myself that he could give me the love and support that I hadn't had from my father.

Secondly: as an able-bodied adult, whether you're a man or a woman, you must avoid relying on anyone else to care for you. It brings out the worst in them, and it hurts you. You have to stand on your own feet: emotionally, socially, financially. That's what this book's about. Bossing UP!

PART 2

SELF

'Learning to love yourself is
the greatest love of all.'

—Whitney Houston

4

SELF-LOVE

The person who must really believe
you're good enough is YOU.

AFRICA HAS PRODUCED THOUSANDS OF FOR-
midable women, but for various reasons, men are far more likely to
be self-assured from the start. In our society, heterosexual men are
valued more than women. Educated boys grow up feeling that they
are entitled to make change happen—to employ people, to lead, and
invent, and drive controversial projects despite opposition.

Educated girls are taught to obey, to look pretty, to have babies,
and cook. Young women may be qualified lawyers or pharmacists,
but they will still not receive the immediate respect that men do or,
very often, equal pay. In most African homes, women and girls are
not permitted in any way to argue, challenge, rebut, refute, offer an
alternative view, or generally stray from the customs and practices
that men have chosen for us. And we can't look to our mothers or
grannies for support. In their day, respect could only be achieved by
compliance, so they are often hostile to defiant girls.

So we usually start from a low base, and when we want to be politicians, and actresses, and inventors, and engineers, and doctors—to make change happen—we have to be twice as good at those things, twice as assertive, while at the same time look pretty, have babies, and cook (and, as the dancer said, doing it all backwards and in high heels).

Does a brilliant, well-paid career, while having a family too, seem impossible? Well, it isn't. Women in other parts of the world and in Africa do it; we just have to seize the advantages they have. One of those advantages is men who are not afraid of female high achievers. A lot of Western men—older ones, especially—can be just as dismissive about women's intelligence and strength as most African men are. But change is gradually happening. And in a way, African women are lucky. We have big extended families who may be able to help. That's much less likely in the USA or in Europe, where women rarely have a network of relations within reach to support her goals.

A lot of expectations will have to change before women are respected the way men are. Every one of us must change the climate around herself.

It all starts with you.

Too many of us look for validation from men, or from other people generally. We feel inadequate unless somebody else boosts our confidence. The person who must really believe you're good enough is YOU. If you don't like your own company, or if you doubt yourself, people will patronize you because you'll draw attention to your self-perceived flaws. 'Oh, I wish I could wear that, but I'm too fat for it' invites an unspoken, irritable 'Don't eat so much then.' Or 'Oh, I couldn't do that. I'd be no use at it' turns your back on possibilities without even bothering to explore them. We have enough barriers without adding our own.

Insecure people look to lovers for comfort. ('Tell me you love me!') You will never get the uncritical, unconditional, perfect love you seek from boyfriends. They have themselves to look after as well.

Insecure people want to fit in with the crowd, or they focus on impressing others. Even those lucky enough to become stars may leave their real friends behind in favour of a crowd of gossiping liggers and hangers-on. Even more women succumb to family pressure. I remember one young woman who was reduced to tears by her own grandmother (as she reduced her village to jaw-dropping silence when she arrived in a Ferrari driven by an Arab prince). Her grandmother chastised, 'You're not married yet? I won't be here forever! When am I going to have grandchildren?'

Nothing obliges you to spend your whole life doing the bidding of your family, trying not to cause offence, or buying friendship. Your achievements, your looks, are enough. If you're genuinely uncomfortable with yourself, make improvements. But don't change because of a request from anybody. Some choices are yours alone to make; so Boss Up.

Exploit whatever makes you unique. I'll give you an example from my life. As a woman, I have a womanly silhouette, but as a little child I was tall and skinny as a stick. I knew this, because I used to get, 'Hey, here comes the stringy chicken!' from a bunch of boys I had to pass every day on my way to primary school. *Agric* was the word they used. And yes, I know it was just a bonding tactic—by picking on me, the only girl, they all bonded together. But it made me ashamed of my appearance.

Then the worst happened. One day we were all told to describe our best friend in front of the class. My friend came out and said, 'The name of my best friend is Chika Ike. She is a teeny girl. A thin girl'.

Well. If I'd been in Texas, it would have been a compliment. Where I came from, it wasn't. I cried. I felt like a freak. Everybody called me The Thin Girl after that. But I couldn't change it, so in the end I exploited it. I grew up slim and tall, so clothes looked good on me. I was able to earn my own money as a model by the time I was sixteen.

It all starts with you.

The person who must really believe you're good enough is YOU.

5

EMBRACE YOURSELF

Feed a misery with attention
and it GROWS. Don't do it!

YOU MIGHT THINK THAT A FILM ACTRESS IS totally self-assured every minute of the day.

Yeah, right.

Believe me, I know my strengths and limitations. I know that ultimately, we are all alone. I know that my happiness depends on my work and my outlook.

Starting a career is a challenge for each of us, and if you are burdened with feelings of inferiority—a suspicion that you are less worthy than your siblings, less desirable than your husband's girlfriend, and without a doubt, stupid (or even borderline crazy)—you easily become nervous and insecure.

The public saved me. I kept acting, in spite of verbal and physical abuse at home, because I was popular. People seemed to like my movies, and I liked having an independent space where I felt wholly me. As long as I was in demand, I could get out of the house and go to work, instead of sitting at home being told I was rubbish. Reviewers were kind, and they gave me constructive criticism as well as praise. I could hold my head high.

I can take constructive criticism! Anyone who wants to try her best needs to learn from honest feedback about her successes as well as the areas for improvement. No one deserves belittling or dehumanizing 'feedback,' either from strangers on the street, friends, family, or your spouse. And with the passage of time, I was able to listen to the voice inside me that said, 'Enough!' After divorce, I learned how to be single and lead a happy life. Even my little dog was happier.

Then Facebook, Instagram, Twitter, and the rest entered my life. Because my career demanded that I keep a high profile, social media were essential. But these spaces of communication can be grabbed by negative influences and turned against any one of us. We may quickly discover that there are people out there who absolutely loathe us! They may hate your voice, your walk, your bum, your height, your hairstyle, your clothes, your associates. They'll make up disgusting lies about you (thereby causing even more people to criticise your skin, your moral judgment, your taste in men, your shoes... and on and on).

You have doubts. You are distressed. You have days when you think you're absolutely hopeless. Why didn't somebody tell you sooner?

I could say that this is only a problem for me because I am a celebrity, but sadly this isn't just happening to me. It can happen to anyone. Even the youngest and most vulnerable among us. Children everywhere—including all those girls with secret ambitions to become midwives and writers and gold medalists at the Olympics— get poisonous online abuse from other children. It is horrible; worse than anything that could ever have happened to me at school. In some countries, young people have been driven to suicide from terrible, hurtful antagonism inflicted through social media.

It is BULLYING.

How should we deal with it?

Analyse, accept, and let go. Trolls who are unkind from behind the screen of the internet are cowards, and they know it. Internet trolls lack confidence in themselves, so they obsess about bringing other people down. They are tragic individuals. If you discover that someone who is harassing you online is a work colleague or school friend (those strange-looking Instagram handles with no followers and few posts... I see you), there's not much you can do except confront that person in real life. And always remember, the internet trolls and the trolls in your life who hide behind a fake handle won't be around you in a few years' time. They will fail. And you will move on to lead a more interesting life than they will ever know. How do I know that? Because cowards never soar. They will eventually fade out of your story, so just ignore them.

If you really can't, just close your accounts. Yes, I know that for most people under 25, that's like living with a bucket over your head, but it's doable, and you can reopen correspondence with the outside world when the trolls are tired and have gone away.

For people like me, participation in social media is a tool of the trade and a vital business activity. I'm a tender flower, but if trolls bother me I can work out for myself whether they're a lone extremist or genuinely offended people. I can analyse their antagonism and figure out why it exists. It's helpful to know if I have misjudged something or made a joke that offended people.

Reading pure spite would just undermine my confidence, so I use the BLOCK button for its intended purpose. My job since early childhood has been building self-confidence, and though such challenges as a child were hard and often painful, the skills I learned serve me well now.

The first lesson I learned was not to take myself too seriously. Nobody is all perfect, or all bad. While we can change our attitudes about ourselves and other people, we have to live with and accept the looks and brains we were born with.

Of course girls want to be desirable. So do men. But girls often measure themselves against actresses and models in magazines who have to pretend to be desirable, like normal women, but astonishingly so. Perfect, in fact. Which none of us is. Photoshop and other software editing programs are routinely used to make celebrities look slimmer and fitter and more flawless than they are. Their fingernails and hair are never allowed to be less than perfect. Fat legs are sculpted to perfection by the computer program, and given a sheen. And loads of actors have chronic skin conditions such as acne. A filter over the lens makes them perfect.

Which brings me to a sensitive subject.

MY PIMPLE.

My pimple was for many years a significant pro blem. Don't laugh. You are about to find out how I was brought down to earth with a loud crash as my self-absorption shattered into a thousand fragments and was replaced by happiness and relief.

Like zillions of teenagers, I got spotty. I had very oily skin. The pimples went away eventually, of course. Except for a scattering on my nose. They stayed. My mom said, 'Mm, they'll go. I had that when I was your age. They went away.'

Well, they did. They went. Then every year at the same time, they came back. First one, then two, then three, four, five—and by then I was a model. And I had my first part in a film. And eventually, my pimples and I (it was that kind of relationship, we went everywhere together) went to London! By that time I had googled to the ends of the internet with the word *pimple*, and I decided I might have sebaceous hyperplasia. (Wow.) I went to a Harley Street dermatologist who he told me yes, that was what it was. Or maybe even rosacea.

'Because that's what happens with pimples on a nose,' he said, sadly. 'It could be one thing or another, and to treat it, we have to give the correct diagnosis.' I couldn't stay for tests so he sent me on my way with ointment. Which didn't work.

What did I try next? What didn't I try! Scrubs. Creams. Lotions made out of exotic herbs. Steroids. Antibiotics. Laser treatment. Snake venom. All right, I made that last one up. But you get my drift.

It (yes, there was only one pimple now) was getting care and attention 24/7. Ticket to an exotic location? I would be googling local dermatologists before I even packed my suitcase. It was like, 'Can't visit the Eiffel Tower/Parthenon/Pyramids this afternoon, I have an appointment.' I should have written a travelogue on the amenities and décor of dermatologists' offices located in the world's most exciting tourist destinations.

This went on for years until one time I found myself in the office of an NYC dermatologist. I was missing, I think, a Christmas show at the Rockefeller Centre.

'How can I help you, Miss Ike?'

'It's my nose.'

He looked at me curiously. His face was at most three feet from mine, and he was wearing glasses.

'What's wrong with your nose?'

'I have this thing—on my nose.'

He leaned forward and stared. He stared, and stared. He leaned back in his chair, and he said, 'You're vain.'

I said, 'What d'you mean, vain?'

'You want to be perfect. Yes, there's a blemish, but it isn't that bad. Why are you focusing on your faults? It's all in your mind.'

'No!' I said. 'I see it in my movies. I see it in pictures in magazines. I see it everywhere.'

He said, 'I'm going to return your consultation fee. There's nothing to treat. It's never going to go away. You just have to live with it.'

So once I got over the shock, I did.

That's the lesson. Accept or adapt, but don't obsess. Embrace your flaws. As soon as I stopped remembering to anoint and examine that damned spot, something magical happened. I had mental space left over that I filled with something more productive. And at that point, the pimple started to shrink on its own.

Feed a misery with attention, and it GROWS.

Don't feed the misery.

Feed a misery with attention and it GROWS. Don't do it!

6

IMPROVE YOURSELF

You learn judgment, trust, values, and
opinions just by living with other people.

A PRODUCTIVE LIFE IS NEVER ABOUT WORK–
eat–sleep. A productive life is about learning. You learn good judgment, trust, values, and opinions by living with other people.

But what about culture? Education doesn't end when you leave
school. It's up to you to stay curious and find stuff out. As our country gets richer, and changes happen faster, there will be many devel-
opments, and that means having enough education to understand
what's happening and keep ahead of the game—in every way. We
must continue to learn as long as we take a breath.

You can use whatever is available to learn new things. The lit-
eracy rate for girls in my country is poor. There's a saying, 'If you
want to keep a secret, put it in a book.' But you're reading this, so you
probably have good English, an education, and access to quite a lot
of books. Also, to the internet. (YAY! for the internet.)

Type a question into Google, and you can find out just about everything you ever wanted to know. How your brain works? It's there, animated and in colour. How many naira to the euro today? Easy. A TED talk on happiness? There are loads on YouTube. What was the Reformation? Does Beyoncé have a pimple too?

The internet is good and bad, like everything else. You can probably find pictures of your old maths teacher naked and drunk, if you look hard enough. (Please don't. Online porn and violence are for saddos, and lies and fake news are out there too.)

If you have a smartphone or a computer, you can learn facts, read, and broaden your mind. The more you research and read, the more confident you get. You might be curious about the Pharoahs or raï or geopolitics or above all else, Your Hair—doesn't matter; having good general knowledge gives you authority and more ideas. The internet can show you how to make a business plan or train as a veterinarian or clean the sink with baking soda and vinegar. You can even learn basic French or German and how to code, for free. Curiosity is good. Stay curious.

You learn judgment, trust, values, and opinions just by living with other people.

7

REASSURE YOURSELF

'I am perfect even in my imperfections.
Those imperfections make me unique.'

NOW FOR SOME ROUTINES; JUST A REMINDER, before we carry on. You need to practise self-confidence. Work at it, constantly reinforce it, until you project positivity when you walk into a room.

You can write on your mirror: 'You're beautiful. You're kind. You have a good heart. You're charitable, strong, fearless. You can do this.' You'll be sure to read that every day if it's posted where you brush your teeth.

Or, right now, stretch your hands out in front of you. Cross your hands to your shoulders and give yourself a tight HUG. Say, 'I am perfect even in my imperfections. Those imperfections make me unique. I look in my mirror, and I love myself. I am so proud of my very being.'

Or if you prefer to recite a golden oldie each morning: 'Every day, in every way, I'm getting better and better.'

You have to love yourself. Say the words again.

Never let your flaws define you. Boss Up! Remember all the positive attributes that you'll demonstrate today. Negative thoughts lead to depression. Depression leads to self-absorption. Self-absorption leads to despair. Despair leads to loss. It all starts with you.

'I am perfect even in my imperfections. Those imperfections make me unique.'

8

TRUST YOUR INSTINCTS

Paying attention to almost-subconscious
warnings is trusting your instincts.

IF IT WALKS LIKE A DUCK AND IT QUACKS LIKE
a duck, it's a duck.

A friend from my childhood shared my house for a long time.
She was working and taking exams and she had a sick mother, so I
helped out with her education and some hospital bills as well. She
became almost like a sister, really, because we'd known each other so
long. She knew my friends, my boyfriend, some of my family, and
some of the people I worked with.

Anyhow, after about a year, she told me she was chasing a job in
Abuja, and for the next few weeks she'd be staying at her sister's place
over there. Something… what was it? I don't know, maybe phone
calls she ended hurriedly, conversations we no longer had, but something made me wonder a little about her story. I didn't tell her that

I'd be filming in Abuja soon, but I asked her to give me her sister's address so that I could send a package.

She'd been gone a week or more when I had to go to Abuja for work. My suspicions were slight, almost under my radar. I didn't think she'd have anything to hide. Nonetheless I decided to pay her a surprise visit.

I was driven to a pleasant suburb with detached houses set back from the road. The car arrived at the right address around 9 pm, and my driver got out in the dusk and told the intercom he had a parcel for her. Lights were on upstairs.

After a delay she came out, in shorts and a tank top as if she'd just got out of bed. She opened the gate to the driver.

'Hi! I've come to see you!' I said and got out of the car. Her smile disappeared, and she looked confused.

'But I didn't know you were in Abuja.'

'Yes, we're shooting here for a few days so I thought I'd surprise you. I don't really know your life here. I thought I'd drop over and meet you all, but have you gone to bed already?'

Expressions of joy and welcome? No. I waited expectantly. She started talking in a distracted way about her family being away and what they were doing.

She still hadn't asked me in.

'Listen,' I said, 'I need to pee. Can I just use your bathroom?'

'No. Sorry, you can't go inside.'

'Why not?'

'I can't... it's not possible right now.'

There was a silence between us. Then I said, 'You stayed in my house for two years rent free, and now you won't let me in to use the toilet?'

'No. You can't go in.'

Behind her a light went on, and the front door opened. I knew that silhouette.

My boyfriend came out to the gate. My boyfriend who'd said he was travelling for a couple of months. Instead he'd rented this suburban love-nest to share with my friend.

He was dumped, with some harsh words, that night. I was hurt and angry but not tremendously surprised; our affair had run its course anyway. The person I felt betrayed most by was the woman who'd taken advantage of my generosity and friendship. After I went back to Lagos I got tearful calls from her—even from her family—about how sorry she was, and would I ever forgive her, and blah blah.

I did forgive her, but I will never trust her again. Although we still talk occasionally, I don't see her. I don't want her around anymore.

And yet, I had been just a little suspicious because I'd subconsciously noticed a wariness in her, weeks before. I should have paid closer attention. Because I didn't, I'd been almost complicit in being deceived.

Paying attention to your almost subconscious warnings is trusting your instincts. We're animals. A cat can't tell you how he knows you're going to feed him, but he's learned the signs: the change in your voice, the way you go to the same place in the kitchen or the yard. When we were children, we were just as acute. We could tell at once if a parent was angry and suppressing it; we observed the tiny facial muscles, the way their eyes don't smile. All children rely on their instincts. As adults we do the same thing, but now we have a contradictory voice inside telling us we're wrong. 'No! She wouldn't do that. How can I even think it?'

Listen, watch, and trust your instincts. Be silent and knowing, like a cat.

Paying attention to almost-subconscious warnings is trusting your instincts.

9

ERASE YOUR FEAR

Accept that you'll sometimes make
a fool of yourself and lie awake
reliving the embarrassment.

IT'S NORMAL TO BE SCARED: FRIGHTENED OF making a fool of yourself, frightened of being poor, frightened of rejection. There are strategies to conquer all these fears.

Accept that you will sometimes make a fool of yourself and lie awake reliving the embarrassment. If you have a memory that recurs and bothers you, try playing the event forwards, like a film, in your mind's eye on an imaginary cinema screen. Then play it backwards. Then backwards faster. Then backwards faster still. See? Do it over again as many times as you can. It works.

Your biggest fear might be lack of money. Poverty means too little independence. That used to be one of my worries too. It should never be a fear, but a motivation. Let it motivate you towards earning and saving. Your strategy is: work. Of course, work alone is never enough. Know any rich, privileged cleaners? But if you face the world with a smile and a willing heart, you'll make progress. You'll have to work as hard as you can, even have several jobs at once. Try to develop every job into something better, by analysing what else needs doing and getting it done. Employers notice. If yours doesn't, then be bold and take your skills elsewhere until you start to climb.

Enlist all the help you can from everyone you know; you'll find friends or family to look after your children, you'll find people you know who want some work done, you might even draw up a business plan and borrow money to start a small legitimate business. As a girl, I earned money by working in my mother's call centre, and later by modelling, and at Lagos University I bought shoes abroad to sell to my friends. I was lucky. I had an education and just enough self-confidence, so I didn't have to scrub public toilets. I didn't earn enough to become properly independent either, but the worry lessened. The worst that could happen would be a dull job—and if I did that dull job brilliantly, there would be an opportunity to find my direction in the end.

I was able to move from modelling to acting because I didn't mind rejection too much. Actors have to audition, remember? Most of us are more likely to be turned down for a part than to get it. I could usually audition without nerves because I'd gained self-confidence in front of an audience when I was still at school. Like most teenage girls I used to under-estimate my own ability. In secondary school I was not always top of the class but a good student, in the top ten of about forty pupils. But I was shy. I wasn't an attention-seeker.

So when I was nominated to be Senior Prefect I was terrified. I knew I'd have to conduct assembly. What if everybody giggled?

I was called in to see my teacher. The final choice was between me and another girl. She looked at me kindly. 'I wonder how you'd cope, Chika. You'll have to project authority, you see. You are calm and quiet, and you give the impression that you wouldn't hurt a fly.'

She was right. I was tall and motherly, but I wasn't aggressive. In my dreams, I would have loved to be Senior Prefect, it would be an honour; but when it stood right there for the taking, it felt like a nightmare. I wanted to swim, but I didn't dare jump into the water.

I went to a Catholic school. The announcement was made in Hall, the following day: Chika Ike would be Senior Prefect. And would I please go to the staff room before my first class?

Timidly I entered the staff room.

'Hallo, Chika. Congratulations! Now, we all have classes so… I have to remind you that you'll be taking service on the assembly ground tomorrow. That's fine with you?'

'What? Tomorrow?'

'Well, yes. You know what the Senior Prefect has to do, Chika.'

My stomach turned over. This meant giving a short sermon. Twenty-four hours from now I would have to command the attention of the whole school. I must have looked horrified.

'Don't worry, dear. I'm sure you'll rise to the occasion. Now, back to your classroom!'

I spent the day tied up in knots of anxiety. At home, Mommy was happy for me. She was used to speaking in front of a big congregation. She smiled.

'Stop worrying, Chika! The more you think about it, the more mistakes you'll make. You have to make some, or you'll never learn anything. But don't worry, you notice your own mistakes far more than other people do. You have to remember that everybody else is leading their own life. Your performance is not their big opportunity to pick on you; it's a new thing for you, but it's just half an hour in their day. They'll take your competence for granted.'

She was right, but all the same I stayed up late making notes about what I'd say. Did you know that after spiders and snakes, public speaking is the number one fear of just about everybody? I went to bed, but I didn't sleep. I got up at dawn and arrived at school at 5:30 am. I was the only person there. I walked up and down on the stage practising what I would say and do.

What if my English is all wrong? What if they don't laugh when they should? What if people just sit silently like dummies? Or if they jeer at me? Or if they whisper and snigger?

Run, said the coward in me. I don't have to do this. I can go home and say I'm ill. If I stay and do it, I'll be ill anyway.

But I was here, now. And suffering from lack of sleep. So I went back to the classroom, sat at a desk, and tried to doze off with my head on my arms.

A short time later, people started turning up.

'Hey, Chika! We're looking forward to hearing you!' I tried to look pleased, but the more enthusiastic they got, the more anxious I felt.

The bell clanged. Everybody headed out to the assembly ground. I got to my feet, and my knees felt wobbly.

The field was filling up fast. Then it was full. I climbed onto the stage. The head teacher introduced me and sat down. I looked towards the back of the crowd. The only way was forwards. I got a grip. When I finished, everybody was calling me preacher! I got applause.

I killed my stage fright that day. I had risen to the occasion. My hands stopped shaking in the first few minutes, and nowadays, I speak in public with far less nervousness. I bossed up!

Many famous actors never get over stage fright. They get it every time, but somehow it goes right away when they start to perform. Since courage is overcoming fear, you have to have fear in the first place. Fear is unavoidable. Either you confront the things that scare you—you stand up and fight—or you run away.

We all have a fight-or-flight control deep in our brains. Stimulated by a crisis, it makes our body release adrenalin so we get extra oxygen to the blood. This can make us stronger and faster for a short time. People who've seen car crashes have been able to lift cars with their bare hands to release the injured, simply because adrenalin makes them fight their fear. That's why I like to tell myself, 'Do it tired, do it scared, do it confused. Just do it!'

On the other hand, if a tiger came around the corner I'd go into flight mode. I'd tear off in the opposite direction faster than a jet plane. (You stay and fight if you want. I know my limitations.)

Accept that you'll sometimes make a fool of yourself and lie awake reliving the embarrassment.

10

LEAVE YOUR COMFORT ZONE

Stretch yourself and avoid the fear.
Don't speak of it or think of it.
Shut it down.

ACHIEVING, BY DEFINITION, MEANS LEAVING your comfort zone. Your comfort zone is static; it's what you know you can do. Achievement means doing better than ever before, when there is an enormous prize to be won—or doing something completely new, which scares you more than anything. It's cold out there. It's uncomfy. But you have to stretch your idea of what's possible. There will be pressure, deadlines, fear. Those things are part of our existence on earth. We're not stones, destined to lie still. We're animals who have to hunt to survive, to thrive.

Stretch yourself and avoid the fear. Don't speak of fear or think of fear. Remember, don't feed the misery (and fear is a form of misery). Shut that fear down.

One day soon after I'd been divorced, my publicist rang to tell me I'd been asked to appear on a TV talk show. I knew I'd be free on the day, so I asked for details. When she told me which show it was I nearly dropped the phone.

'No WAY. Not him. He interviews people live. And it's for a whole half hour. Oh, no. I mean, it'll be all about the divorce, won't it?'

'Well, yes—that will be part of it—'

'It'll be like going through the whole thing again. And I've never met him… we might hate each other, so I'll probably freeze or burst into tears or something—'

'You have to do it,' she cut in. 'This is a threshold moment.'

'A what?'

'A moment when a new door opens and you go through it. No matter what. Come on, Chika—there's nothing to worry about.'

I sincerely hoped that my dress would get burned by an asteroid. Or that the night before, the producer would happen to run into Femi Kuti and reschedule… but, no. The publicist didn't ring to say it was cancelled.

Early evening on the day, I hoped for a major traffic jam.

The jam cleared. We arrived at the TV station. It's live. It's live….

In my head, I heard my mother's voice, 'Stop feeding your fear.'

I sat in the studio, in front of the audience, under the lights, and faced my interviewer. He interviewed. I talked. We laughed.

People were really nice.

I thought, *Is that it? Is that what kept me awake?* I could do it again the next day.

Ask yourself: If it doesn't kill you, will it make you stronger? And if you say the wrong thing, will anybody else care very much?

Whatever happens—Boss Up to the challenge.

Stretch yourself and avoid the fear. Don't speak of it or think of it. Shut it down.

11

CONTROL YOUR THOUGHTS

If you feed positivity, it thrives and leads to positive action and true happiness.

I DON'T LIKE USING WELL-WORN CLICHÉS, BUT here is one that can't be better expressed: 'If you think you can, or if you think you can't, either way, you're right.' In other words, your thoughts will become self-fulfilling prophecies. Your attitudes have outcomes. Positive attitude, positive outcome. Negative attitude, no result at all.

Two thousand years ago Epictetus summed it up. 'It isn't events themselves that disturb people, but only their judgments about them.' Half a glass of water is set before two thirsty people. One rejoices at the sight of a glass half full of water; the other despairs, since the glass is already half empty.

Most people still don't get it. What's so difficult?

If you think you'll succeed, you will; if you think you'll fail, you will.

If you both think your marriage is on the rocks, you're already on your way to divorce court. If you're both certain it can be saved, you'll make sure it will be saved.

Your attitude to life is more powerful than anything. It can spur you to success or derail you. As a man thinketh, so he becomes. Many positive thinkers believe their attitude brings the Law of Attraction into play. Try positive thinking and affirmations of the kind I showed you in Chapter 7 ('Reassure Yourself'), and you will find that you are focusing on the best in yourself and the brightest possible view of the world beyond. Other people will be attracted to that, probably because your smiling face is irresistible and makes them feel better, too. As yet another cliché tells us, 'Laugh and the world laughs with you; cry and you cry alone.' Perfectly true. Have you ever spent a whole afternoon with somebody who's really, really glum? I have. I came away convinced that the whole world was awful, everyone in it was a liar or a cheat, and this dismal life was barely worth living.

That attitude for me didn't last, and it won't be repeated. I have practised positive thinking for years. When I stumble over a pothole in life's road, do I just sit there and wail? I look on the bright side. The road's still sunny, the trees are green, and no tigers are coming. I've just got to pick myself up and get moving again.

I shall tell you when I recognised the importance of this. I was on a film set, working on my final scene of the shoot. The actor who played my boyfriend was supposed to give me a violent shove after a heated argument.

'Action!' called the director.

The actor stepped forward and pushed. I was suddenly off balance, and we all heard a loud crack. I screamed as I hit the floor. The pain was excruciating. I was wincing and moaning. The actor was horrified and helpless at the same time. The director shouted for a First Aid box. His assistant rushed off to look for it. Everybody crowded around, giving opinions. The director was kneeling and trying to massage my leg. He meant well, but it was my toes that hurt, and the massage was making them feel worse.

I gasped. 'It's not my leg. It's not my leg! It's my toes, on that foot… the first four toes. OOOO. Owwww! It's agony. I think I must have dislocated something. OOO. Please don't touch… I'll be fine.'

I had to be fine.

I got home. I was still married then. I couldn't sleep that night. The pain in my foot made me cry into my pillow. I turned, gingerly, onto my back, eyes wide open. I made myself stop crying. I had months of work ahead, piles of scripts to read, and I was due on another film set in five days.

'The secret of success is turning up.' Woody Allen, the film director, said that, and I believed it. My foot was swollen and I couldn't drive, but I did turn up. I asked the director to avoid long shots where it would show. He was kind enough to do that.

Two months later the swelling had reduced, but my foot was still agonising so I made an appointment at the Orthopedic Hospital. The doctor stuck a shadowy X-ray onto a screen.

'How long have you been putting up with this? You've got four fractured metatarsals. See, there, your toes?'

He indicated ugly white lines across the monochrome image of my toe-bones. He asked me when it had happened, and I told him.

'Well, you've done all the wrong things, and I don't know how on earth you've managed to endure the pain. Those breaks need time to heal.'

'But I've got to—'

'No buts. You have to keep that foot off the ground, and rested. When you are able to walk, you must not wear heels. It will probably take two years for those fractures to heal properly.'

He sent me to see a nurse, and my foot and lower leg were encased in plaster of Paris. As the doctor handed me crutches, he said, 'You'll be using these for at least eight months.'

I was devastated.

My career was on the rise; I couldn't turn down these opportunities. They wouldn't come again. And what about my finals next month?

My mum came to visit me at home. My husband was at work. She did her best, but I had made up my mind that my situation was disastrous. I was useless. I couldn't even help myself. Several times, after my husband had gone to work, I tried to clamber heavily downstairs to the kitchen to get something to eat, but in my hopelessness I faltered and fell, only to land at the bottom of the stairs. I stayed there, hour after hour, without even the will to get up. I used to lie there until my husband came back from work, knowing that he would help me back onto my feet and guide me and my weighty plastered leg up the steps and back to bed. I could do nothing without help. I was an invalid.

I could have given classes called 'Think Yourself Unhappy,' but I was too unhappy.

One morning I woke up and Bossed Up. I decided that if this was rock bottom, I'd had enough. Self-pity was stupid. From now on, I would reject thoughts that kept me helpless on the floor (literally and figuratively). To make that easier, I would get out of this situation. I called my mum and asked her to take me back to the hospital. I was going to have the plaster taken off.

'You're crazy, Chika. You shouldn't do this.'

'Please, Mum.'

'OK. I don't like it... but if you say so. They're your toes. It's your choice.'

Looking exasperated, she drove me there. I told the doctor I was having some kind of skin reaction, it was all too much to bear, and so on. He agreed that the plaster could be taken off in such a way that I would be able to wash the leg and foot, then replace the plaster and apply a band that would secure it to my leg.

So I came hobbling out to my mother's car quite happy. I knew I could take the thing off again once I got home, and I intended to keep it off. I was sure my leg would heal in no time. I felt instantly hopeful.

I was still in pain, but I started driving myself to school for my exams. I still used the crutches to keep my weight off my injured foot, and when the exams over, I started accepting movie work again. I couldn't act on crutches, but I focused on positive thoughts and images of my healed toes, and got through just fine. Four months later I was pain-free. Back at the Orthopedic Hospital, the foot was X-rayed and all four metatarsals were healed.

This is the power of positive thought. My thoughts conditioned my body to heal fast, and God used my faith to heal me completely, long before the eight months the doctor had predicted would be necessary.

Your thoughts affect your situation, so be self-aware and don't allow negative thoughts to creep in. Please don't wallow in despair. If you feed negativity, it feeds depression and can lead to addiction. If you feed positivity, it thrives and leads to positive action and true happiness. There is so much good in your life. Count those blessings.

The mind-body link is how faith healing works. Believe you're well, behave as if you're well, and your mental energy makes that happen. When I stopped feeding my obsession with that stupid pimple, the problem dwindled. When I believed my toes would be fine, they were. Thinking positively, appreciating the world around you, and focussing on hope, makes yours a happier, more productive life.

If you feed positivity, it thrives and leads to positive action and true happiness.

12

BE PROUD
OF YOUR
INTELLECT

Whatever you do,
broaden your understanding

I KEEP MY AIMS IN VIEW BY SAYING THEM
aloud, in private. For five years I said to myself, 'I will study at
Harvard.'

Harvard Business School has always been a dream of mine. I
had a degree, but I wanted to understand business. There was every
reason to head for the top, and Harvard Business School ranks
among the best schools of its type in the world. After five rejections,
I got in.

I travel a lot and work while I'm on the move. So after my second module, I was on a flight back to Nigeria sitting beside the managing director of a multinational oil company. A Frenchman. We
were talking. He asked me what I did for a living.

'I'm an actress,' I said. 'In films.'

'Oh, really? So how's the film industry doing in Nigeria?'

I told him it was doing well.

He had nothing much to say to me after that. I carried on with my work, which was an academic assignment, which had Harvard's name at the top of the screen.

He saw this. 'You're doing work with Harvard?'

'Yes, I'm at Harvard Business School.'

He closed his laptop and turned to engage me in conversation. We talked for about an hour.

There are several lessons in this story.

First: film and fashion are great topics, but not enough. Whatever you do, broaden your understanding, because in the course of a given day you may meet people who feel passionate about anything from Aikido to Zoology. At the very least, you can listen and ask questions.

Second lesson: you have no idea what people are interested in until they tell you. However, almost everyone is somewhat interested in business. Ask at any airport bookstore and you'll find that, faced with an intercontinental flight in first class, people of both sexes buy books about business. They are also quite likely to read about economics, finance, politics, ethics, science and technology, environmental challenges.... Dig into the ongoing issues that spark interest in you, and knowing the basics gives you self-confidence in difficult situations and a way to connect with just about anyone. Watch the news and look for online articles from magazines like *New Scientist* or *The Economist*; find TED talks that interest you. When you're sixteen, politics and science may be of no interest whatsoever. When you get to 26, you're starting to recognise that they impact your personal life every single day. By 36, your understanding may take you places you never dreamed of.

There are other lessons. But now it's time for revision. You already know about sleep and diet-and-exercise and probably hear a health guru talking about leafy green vegetables or vitamins on YouTube at least once a week.

Know what? I don't care to rehash the same old advice! I want to share with you the next couple of life lessons because our health is directly related to and can be threatened by our lifestyles. If you are tired and unhealthy, you are losing.

Whatever you do, broaden your understanding

13

ZZZZZ...
TAKE
A BREAK

You have to be punctual.
And WIDE AWAKE.

A CERTAIN AMOUNT OF STRESS IS NORMAL.
Mine clearance experts and brain surgeons have two of the hardest jobs on the planet, but they know what they're doing. So although they risk their lives or someone else's every day, that enormous responsibility is what they're trained to carry.

The rest of us have bullying bosses, money worries, trolls, deadlines—one thing after another. Tiring, and mostly unnecessary, and we don't seem to have been trained to cope with life's minor crises at all.

Worry can ruin your life. I've learned to de-stress every day. Take ten minutes: shut your eyes, listen to music, or listen to the room. Don't think about your family or your partner or the price of fish. Just enjoy being alive. Count your blessings. Think about anything (unless it creates stress!). Try to rest in a clear, uncluttered environment with some flowers or elements of nature around.

Rest makes you more productive, and less likely to let the team down, which is crucially important in my business. Film actors can work punishing hours. When decisions are made about when and where to shoot, available light matters. And if you have to be on set at first light, say 6 am, and you didn't get to bed until 3 am, you will darn well turn up regardless. No excuses. If you don't show up for a scene you're supposed to be in, there will be hell to pay—your whole career can be over. The secret of success is showing up. That's true for all of us. Never forget that.

This is why. Let's say a director with an idea for a low-budget, independent film spends her own money getting a passable script together. She takes her idea for the film and her draft script and her proposed budget to all the financial backers (producers) that she knows. Time (unpaid) passes. The fifteenth producer says, 'I'm interested.'

He may come up with his own figure for how much it's going to cost to make the film. He hires a new writer to perfect the script, and he goes to his bank. They lend him a few millions to make the film. He goes back to the director. They book all the pre-production and post-production and facilities and crew; they are working towards a shooting date when the actors and locations and everybody necessary for filming will be in place, on set, ready to work. The casting director will discuss the final choice of actors with the director because she and the producer want the film to be taken up by distributors (who put films into cinemas) and make money at the box office, because if it's a hit, the producer will find it easier to raise money for his next film.

Everyone involved is an expert, paid top rates for every minute of their time, so you can see that film-making is expensive, and to make money, the director's plan has to work. Not one minute can be wasted because time is money. If you're filming in a particular location, for instance, some money from the budget has been used to rent the space—whether it's a street scene or a private house, the space has to be rented. On top of that, you've only got the rented space available to use for a certain number of hours. There is a strict schedule so that the next phase (post-production, maybe a month or more away) will start on time; again, all the staff and facilities are pre-booked.

So everything's ready to go, and everybody knows where they have to be, when shooting starts. There will be scores of people on set, all of whom have one specialised job: anything from production manager to camera assistant, sound technician, lighting specialist— they all have their job to do, and they are all ON TIME. At a quarter to six they are all present and setting up the equipment and props ready for filming. Everybody expects the talent (the people who will appear on screen) to be there too. Without us, they can't start. No stand-ins; a famous name among the talent will have helped persuade the bank to invest in the producer, and pre-publicity about the famous name will have piqued interest among distributors and the potential audience.

Imagine, therefore, how popular an actor is if she fails to show up for no good reason. All those people are in place and ready to work—film crew, other actors, caterers, dressers, makeup artists, not to mention equipment hire, location hire… all this still must be paid for regardless if a single scene is shot. The actor who fails to show up could be blacklisted by the producer and never work again in the industry.

A lot of other jobs are less extreme versions of the same thing. You're part of a professional team, and on the day you are expected to work, you have to show up. Most work, from farming to construction through surgery to retail, is teamwork.

Not only do you have to be punctual. But WIDE AWAKE.

Lack of rest can make you ill. Sleep scientists have shown that after a poor night's sleep, children don't learn properly and adults drive as if they were drunk. All of us produce growth-and-repair hormones during the night as we sleep. Teenagers need to sleep between eight and ten hours because they are growing so much—they're not just being lazy.

Here are the seven golden rules for good sleep:

1 Write a to-do list for tomorrow before you go to bed.

2 Don't watch a screen. The blue light it emits will make your brain think it's still daylight. There are apps, and settings on some phones, that change blue light.

3 Eat and drink at least three hours before bed and avoid alcohol and coffee.

4 Sleep at a comfortable temperature.

5 Have a bath or shower just before you sleep.

6 Have a hot drink (with milk if you tolerate it because it makes you sleepy).

7 If you wake up in the night and can't get back to sleep, get up. Do something else for half an hour before you go back to bed, and make time for a twenty-minute doze the following day.

You have to be punctual. And WIDE AWAKE.

14

RUN
YOUR
OWN RACE

Mind your business;
stay focused on your own lane.

STAR QUALITY MEANS BEING NOTICED. IF YOU want to make a memorable impression, the easiest way is to dress outrageously. Unfortunately, I've met plenty of individuals in wacky clothes who turn out to be as interesting as a slab of concrete.

The world's high achievers have all dared to think differently. They've never been lazy enough to drift with the crowd. They've taken a radical new approach that everybody said wouldn't work or that no one had thought of or dared to follow. They've learned the rules of their particular game and how to play it well, and then they've broken the rules and improved the game. This applies in everything from painting, poetry, medicine, engineering, through cosmetics and jazz to Facebook. Lady Gaga wasn't going broke last time I looked, either.

You name it, progress comes when an expert breaks the rules. It takes bravery to stand out from the crowd. At first you'll have to do it without the help of publicists or sponsors. So if you are an influencer, a game-changer, let the world know. You have to believe in yourself, and it's important to make sure that people know that your original ideas are yours. If you don't, people will claim them for their own. Or they'll try to divert you towards their variant of your idea, take control of it—and you—and then suck up the credit.

So mind your business, not other people's, and don't let yourself be underestimated by any label. As an actress, I suffer from stereotyping as someone who has nothing to do except look pretty and learn lines. If only. If you find you're being patronised, be assertive and be yourself. Boss Up.

Although there is an alternative…

Mind your business; stay focused on your own lane.

15

FAKE IT TILL YOU MAKE IT

'Live it, and it becomes your truth.'

A FRIEND OF MINE CHOSE A STEREOTYPE AND fit herself into it. One that would work for her, not against: British, privately educated, sophisticated.

I knew her at secondary school. Even then she had a cut-glass English accent. How? Why? We thought maybe her father was British. But she was not mixed-race. She used to tell us stories about her cousins from London and how she talked with them. You'd think she'd lived there herself. (We used to wonder.) But she insisted she'd never been outside Nigeria. She could even tell you about expensive fragrances, Chanel Number 5 and Amouage Gold, because she had uncles and aunties who wore perfume. And maybe she'd read European magazines.

In secondary school she ate with a knife and fork and laid them side by side diagonally across the plate when she had finished, English style. We really didn't do table manners in that way. Awesome.

However, we couldn't see all this leading to anything so we wrote it off as pretension and we called her a wannabe. When I had lunch with her one day after we'd left school, she was so appropriate and ladylike. I asked her, 'Have you ever been to a school of etiquette?'

'Chika, I've never left Nigeria. I wouldn't even know where to start looking for a school of etiquette.'

'Well, did your cousins teach you—'

'No. Since I was little, I copied them. I don't remember them teasing me about sounding Nigerian, it's just that their way of behaving and talking was very controlled, and I liked that. So I faked it and now it's part of me. I know now that's a technique, but it was instinctive for me as a child because I wanted to be just like them. Ever heard of Fake It Till You Make It?'

'Yes. Live it, and it becomes your truth. That's what you've done, isn't it?'

'I think so. And I watched films to find out how Western girls walk and talk and flip their hair. Americans cut their food up and then switch hands and eat with a fork only, but Europeans eat with knife and fork together.'

'Really? And here's me watching movies for entertainment.'

'Oh, what a waste.' She grinned. 'And if there's a lot of silverware on both sides of the plate, work from the outside in as each course is served. My cousin told me that.'

'What else?'

'What d'you want to know?'

'Umm... look... we have a wine list, right?' I picked it up. 'I hardly ever order wine because I don't know one from another. If I'm out on a date and the guy orders, I'm like, Oh, I'll have what you're having.'

'I can tell you the basics.'

'Oh, please DO!'

Sisters, I took notes. This was stuff I'd always wanted to know, and we were in the Dark Ages before YouTube. Apparently it's red wine with red meat and white wine with fish or white meat, like chicken. If you see dessert wines on a menu, they're really sweet and you only have them with dessert, and if you see liqueurs or brandy, they're for drinking after a meal, often with an espresso.

I wrote as fast as I could. 'So what else?'

'If it's a curry or something, get beer or water. Anything really spicy will make wine taste awful.'

'Okay. You know I'm going to learn all this by heart.'

'And never ever ask for ice with wine. White wine is chilled. Red wine doesn't go in the fridge. You drink it at room temperature.'

'Got that. Why?'

She was really into this. 'The taste. It depends on the grape variety and the place where they're grown. Black grapes are crushed to make red wine from varieties like Merlot and Pinot Noir and Malbec.' (She said 'Mairloh' and 'Peenoh Nwah' like a Parisian.) 'Those need long, hot summers to develop, so they come from places like southern France and Italy or South Africa. They make white wine as well, but the famous white-grape varieties, like Chardonnay or Sauvignon Blanc' (she said 'Soh-vee-nyon blon" and sort of swallowed the sound at the end), 'those do best in cooler places like Germany and northern France. The label shows you the year it was produced, and the grape variety, and where it comes from. Sometimes—especially with the mass-produced, cheaper wines—it's several different kinds of grape, blended, and the label will say so on the back. Those stay the same, year on year. With more expensive wine, the year it was produced makes a big difference to the taste.'

'How do you know all this stuff?'

'I just kept asking my cousins and reading what I could. It's supposed to be, the older the wine the better, but that's not true because some wine gets better, and then worse after a few years, and other wine is made from grapes grown during a cold, wet summer and will never be much good anyway. If it's red wine from a really good year and a famous vineyard, dealers buy it and keep it in a cellar for years until it's super-expensive because it's so good.'

'So it's almost impossible to choose.'

'Yes. But try different ones and stick with what you like. It works for me.'

'Okay, I've got all that. I have to ask. What's an apéritif?'

'It's for drinking before a meal, with olives or nuts or something. Never drink on an empty stomach. That's the rule. Eat something fatty with alcohol, otherwise you'll have one glass of wine and fall over.'

'That's me, exactly! Oh, thank you for the tip.'

'And it's a good idea to drink a glass of water at the same time. The alcohol will affect you less.'

'You are so ladylike.'

'That's another thing. Deportment. You get it from old movies. Watch Audrey Hepburn in *Breakfast at Tiffany's*. There is a way to sit down. And a way to get in and out of a car.'

'Tell me!'

'If you're sitting down, you keep your knees together and cross your ankles neatly to the side. You never cross your knees.'

'Oh.'

'And if you're wearing a skirt, and getting into a car, you slide into the seat backwards and twist towards the front while you swing your legs into the car with your knees together.' She kind of mimed it as she explained it, without (of course) scraping her chair back to show me.

'I'll have to practise.'

'Hey, it's easy. And if you do the same thing in reverse on the way out, you won't mind having your picture taken.'

'I never do.'

'But if you just clamber in and out of a car with your legs all over the place, you can flash your underpants! You really don't want to look like a giraffe with knickers.'

'Okay. I'll promise to be good from now on. Go on, I'm still taking notes.'

'Umm... I was told never to hang my bag on the chair. Always keep it on my lap. It makes sense. It all makes sense, actually.'

Actually! How much more British could she get? That girl acted as the person she wanted to be. She did it so well that she has the career she always wanted, is married to a billionaire's son, has two children, and her dream job. Truly a class act.

Well. I don't believe in deception. And I don't know what your aim in life is. But if all else fails, Fake It Till You Make It. Because you are faking what you most desire for yourself, you're deceiving no one but working toward your most authentic life.

BOSS UP! TO-DO LIST

What do you like about yourself (physical, intellectual, behavior, etc.)?

What do you get complimented about by people around you?

What keeps you awake at night before you sleep?

What are five things you'd love to improve about yourself?

Who do you have around (friend, family, etc.) that can help you reach these improvement goals?

Have you ever internalized someone's negative view about your looks, skills, and attitude? What were those negative views, and why did you believe them?

Do you believe you are capable of achieving your dreams? Why and why not?

Write a love letter to yourself. In it, write everything you love about yourself, write how you have come this far, and write how you are going to achieve your dreams.

'Live it, and it becomes your truth.'

PART 3

| | | | | | | |

BUSINESS

"Nothing will work unless you do."

Maya Angelou

16

AIM FOR THE STARS

Choices that result from success
are good choices to have.

YOU'LL HAVE PERSONAL AND PROFESSIONAL goals if you're not a rock but are a person who wants to live your best life as a constantly growing and learning human being. Using the principle of 'Aim for the stars and at least you'll reach the moon,' each of your goals must seem almost out of reach.

Suppose you want to be a doctor. 'Passing my exams into med school' absolutely, categorically, must NOT be your goal. If it is, you run a serious risk of dropping out of med school because you'll subconsciously feel that you have already hit your mark. You got the exam result, so now… life ahead is a blank.

As long as you focus on one almost-unachievable ambition, you will never drop out. So the exams are just a step on your way to becoming President of the World Medical Association, or a Consultant Neurosurgeon, or setting up a chain of 1000 drop-in surgeries all over Africa. Those achievements require many, many steps, each of which you can plot. A goal worthy of your life and effort will rarely sit straight ahead, unopposed. At each stage there may be temporary hindrances or new strategies requiring decisions. Perhaps you have to re-sit an exam. Or perhaps you've opened 400 drop-in surgeries when you receive an offer to buy your business for millions. Do you take the money, or do you keep heading for your goal of 1000 surgeries, or can you compromise and achieve an even better result?

Of course, your aim may change. You goal is to become President of World Medical, but you discover, over the course of many years' service in the Nigerian Medical Association, that you'd really rather be caring for patients directly. So you go back to doctoring. Because you've actually recognised that the ambition you had resulted in a confrontation with your higher goal: you no longer want to be an important bureaucrat but you recognise that to feel happy and ful-filled, you must leave public life. But at least you gave your goal a chance, learned an important lesson along the way, and remained open to change in a way that honours your highest goals for yourself.

You'll never know what you might have done unless you set up a distant goal and do your darnedest to reach it. Without aspiration, you'll bumble along doing the same old thing and turning into one of those people who hate any kind of change. They don't just sit still, they practically fuse with the chair.

Your loved ones can present a dilemma in your career. Are your children going to take first place if they're settled in school in Lagos, but you've been invited to do your dream job in Abuja? Is your hus-band happy to move? What about your aged parents? You'll have to negotiate your way through all sorts of obstacles, big and small, but choices that result from success are good choices to have. I haven't changed my mind about my goals in life, but I've adapted to changed circumstances and remapped the journey ahead. The more health, wealth, and happiness we have, the easier it is to be adaptable. So Boss Up!

Get out there and earn it.

Choices that result from success are good choices to have.

17

GET A VISION BOARD

Repeat, reinforce, internalise.

YOU ALREADY KNOW ABOUT MY VISION BOOK.
But I also have a vision board—a felt board with a frame about twenty inches by twelve. It's a way of assisting daily focus on life's blessings and possibilities: my family and love life, my career and finances—achieving, giving, learning, making, improving.

The idea is that every time you see your board—with its picture of your lover, the inspirational poem a friend sent you and all the things that speak to your heart—you'll feel happier and more confident. It has images of the blessings you adore. The places you've been to, things that make you laugh, treats you're looking forward to, memories you treasure. And reminders of the wisdom you live by.

It also proclaims images of what you want. If you visualize your goals, you interact with the world in full consciousness of what you want because it's at the forefront of your mind all the time. If you pin a US dollar to the board because you're saving to see your cousin in New York, and an image of the gates to a mansion you'll buy when your profit reaches a certain point—you'll be powerfully motivated.

Sports people use a similar principle. Suppose you're taking tennis lessons. You watch a five-minute video of Serena Williams winning game, set, and match. Watch her again every day, and you will unconsciously absorb the way she moves and reacts and handles the racquet. When your tennis lesson comes round, you're suddenly a better player. You've internalised a message: 'This is how to play tennis.'

The same magic happens with the help of a vision board—repeat, reinforce, internalise. You'll live with the image of those gates; you'll act as if you're ready to move into the mansion that day. You can pin cuttings or pictures or invitations or even mementoes onto a corkboard or a tree, doesn't matter—just post your visuals in a place where you'll see them every day. Change your vision board around regularly so that you never start get bored with it or ignore it.

If you want, you can take a photograph of your vision board for your phone and make it wallpaper or use it as the screenshot on your laptop. That way, during life's pointless voids—waiting for a bus, waiting to pitch for a contract—you lit your output of positivity, confidence, and happiness and radiate it to all who meet you.

Repeat, reinforce, internalise.

18

NEVER GIVE UP

Focus on your plan and stick
with it. It's normal to wobble;
but you cannot look down.

YOU HEAR THIS ALL THE TIME.

As we've seen, the people who stand out are usually those who know what they're doing and have thought of a better way to do it. Nor are they afraid of showing others their way. If you are someone with a vision, you need enormous self-belief, encouragement (if you can get it), and (in my case) faith. Because the more new and different your plan is, the more likely you are to meet opposition.

Here's an example. Until the early 1990s, if you had a terrible pain just above your belly-button that only a glass of milk would cure, your doctor would tell you it was a stomach ulcer, probably stress-related. You'd be sent away with a drug that reduced the pain. There was no cure.

But a couple of Australian doctors proved that most ulcers are caused by bacteria called *Helicobacter pylori*. They knew how to kill off those bacteria. They published their findings. The medical establishment sneered. Impossible! 'Everybody knows you can't cure ulcers,' they said. But the Australians were curing people, despite the naysayers.

So defying suspicion, dismissal, and sheer rudeness from medical professionals all over the world, they kept on treating people, and very gradually their solution became trusted and successful. In 2005 they were awarded the Nobel Prize for Medicine.

If you know that you're right, persist. Ignore the sneers.

Human beings can be almost superhuman. Focus is everything: sheer, dogged determination to be the best at what you do. There's a 2008 film called *Man on Wire*. It's the true story of a French high-wire walker who in 1974 danced across empty sky, on a wire slung between the Twin Towers of the World Trade Centre. Philippe Petit had spent six years perfecting his craft and working out exactly how to do his stunt. He shared his plans with only a handful of helpers because what he wanted to do was illegal.

Crowds stared up as his tiny figure stepped delicately back and forth, 1350 feet above Wall Street, for an hour. I can think of no high-wire achievement that could be more frightening or more difficult. It's cold and windy up there, and the wire would dip and sway and rise.

Focus on your plan and stick with it. It is normal to wobble; but you cannot look down.

By comparison with Monsieur Petit's, my plan was as hard as eating an unripe mango. I had a strong proposal in mind for a reality TV programme that would showcase the talents of young African women. I'd call it *African Diva*. I'd run auditions, and the participants I chose would be taken to an unknown location and judged on certain tasks, and eliminated until only the winner was left. With an idea like that, you'd generally try to interest a production company in making a pilot programme. They'll find sponsors for the pilot and show it to the people at the networks who commission shows, who—if they like it—might greenlight a season of six or eight or twelve episodes. You'll have rights as the originator of the idea, but the production company will have done so much of the preliminary work, including the budget, that they'll have the final say in what the show looks like.

I was determined to set up my own production company so I could keep all the rights to how *African Diva* was made. But guess what? I didn't have enough money. So I reached out to a friend who has always encouraged me. I gave him my pitch. I was bubbling with enthusiasm. I told him what a terrifically empowering thing this would be. So many Nigerian girls have what it takes to be stars. He didn't disagree with me.

'I can see how passionately you feel about this, and I can see why, but Chika, this programme is just not practical. Girls coming to your house to audition? It'll be chaos. You need a controlled environment. A studio. And who are the judges going to be? They're not gonna do it for peanuts.'

With negative bias like that underlying all the responses you're likely to get, you learn to expect a lot of 'no's.' But you can't sell anything unless you believe in your product and are prepared to push until you get a positive answer. Failure is not an option. Somebody will listen and imagine the possibilities with you, rather than reacting with knee-jerk negativity towards something new and different. If not, you'll find another way to make it happen.

I kept asking potential sponsors. It was like pushing a boulder up a hill. After the last refusal, I almost gave up. But I'd come so far, and I still believed in my idea as much as I did the first time I pitched it. The darkest hour comes before the dawn.... I thought of another way.

I stopped asking for backing and started the auditions anyway.

I publicised them. I told the world exactly who I wanted to find and why. I couldn't back out after that. People were paying attention, and the participants were chosen. I had to produce something and get it onto the airwaves. I ended up self-funding a whole first season.

It was a huge success, and I sold the idea to a cable platform. The second season was easier because sponsors were coming to me, and it aired on a terrestrial station with a bigger viewership than before, right across Africa.

My friend called me. He said, 'Wow. You never gave up. I've seen the show. It's amazing. I'm sorry I discouraged you.'

'You didn't,' I said. 'You motivated me. I'm sorry you doubted me, but that was a challenge.'

I'm on my third season now. It's a slow process, growing a show. I have angels (backers), and I hope we can attract more. I challenge myself every day. I have learned to ignore the dream-killers. It's been hard. There have been times when I've wanted to stay in bed and stop trying. Those times are tests: tests of how much I want something and how hard I will fight for it. Anything worthy of pinning to a vision board will come with times where those goals are tested. Expect those challenges to come, and push through.

Often when people discourage you they're not reacting to your proposal or idea so much as to disappointments they've had in the past. All of us are wary of making a move that will lead to disappointment. We all have to make judgements about what to do with our money. If they've made a mistake before in an important decision (who hasn't?), they won't be easy to persuade again. The newer the idea, the bigger the risk. If your goal is truly fresh or ground-breaking, expect at least one no. You probably won't know exactly what drives the negative response, but don't take every rejection personally.

Shrug off a no. Pursue your dreams and don't give up.

Visit to Morocco on an African diva tour to
speak on importance of education

Focus on
your plan
and stick
with it.
It's normal
to wobble;
but you
cannot
look down.

19

MONEY AND EMOTION

Get it in writing, or you won't
be ABLE to Boss Up.

MONEY AND EMOTION ARE A TOXIC MIX.

Suppose you're out of work. A friend says she'd like to help. She'll pay you to organise a big party at her house, with really good food. She hands over the money for food and drink and the hire of silverware and glasses; you agree on a fee for the work. You cook, and you and your sisters fix the drinks and the service. It's at least three days of hard work between the three of you. You've done this sort of thing before, so you go for it with enthusiasm. Your friend thanks you. It was a marvellous party, and you did it so well. She's putting your cheque in the post.

You're relying on your fee to pay your sisters and, just as importantly, your rent. Two days later, party woman has gone overseas, and when she comes back there's still no sign of payment. Three weeks after the party, you call her and you're angry.

Getting angry about money is never a good look. It reveals that you desperately need it. It situates you as the weak one in this transaction. And she knows you're powerless to enforce payment because you bet the farm on her casual verbal promise. You have no agreement in writing. If it went to court (which it won't, because you can't afford to legally chase her for the money), it's your word against hers. And she knows this.

Don't risk getting emotional. If money is involved, even between friends, get it in writing. Make a short, totally clear agreement in advance that both of you can sign and date. And if anyone else produces an agreement or a contract, don't sign and date it without reading it first. Even if it's twenty pages. Read it. If you don't understand it, ask a lawyer, your professional association, or a clued-in friend.

Shall I tell you why I'm so onto this? Two reasons.

Men get angry and shout, but angry women are often frustrated by people not taking their anger seriously. When I'm angry, that sheer, dumb frustration makes me cry. Crying is the last thing you should do in business, because people in the room will say, 'Hey, don't get upset.'

UPSET!!!! AT THAT MOMENT, I FEEL LIKE STARTING NUCLEAR WAR! That's why I'm crying; I don't want to, but I'm a woman, and therefore born without the instinct to punch anyone on the nose.

Crying, in business, is a big losing move. You have to be dispassionate and determined to get what you want, and train yourself to control emotion to channel it into action. If you have a signed agreement, you don't need to argue if you're cheated because your lawyer will be able to put your case in court.

Here's the second reason why I'm onto this written contract thing. Four years ago, a friend, who is a producer/director as well as an actor, called and asked me to dinner, 'Chika, there's something I want to talk to you about.'

Well, we're in the same business, so I decided to give him a listening ear. It might be an opportunity, it might be a dilemma, but what are friends for?

He told me about his great idea for a movie. It was ready to go: script, cast, equipment, locations, crew, everything lined up. He was bubbling with enthusiasm. From what he said, the key roles were all taken, so somewhere at the back of my mind I wondered why he wanted to discuss it with me.

Turned out that the shoot couldn't start because his seed money was all gone and so was the budget for filming. Somehow our conversation turned into a therapy session. He was in tears. He didn't know where to turn, et cetera. His wife was pregnant and his little boy was in the hospital. The doctors' bills were huge. They'd only get through the next few months if he could make this brilliant movie. He had to go forward with it.

He cast himself as a victim of circumstance, and I fell for it. Tears came to my eyes when I thought of his little boy. I sympathised with his pregnant wife. I felt bad for him because he seemed a victim of a pure case of bad luck. Once he'd caught those sympathy signals, he immediately ratcheted up his appeal.

He'd asked me to dinner because I was his last hope. He hated asking. But if anyone could save them all it would be me. Could I? Would I? All he needed was a loan. He'd pay me interest… he needed just enough to tide him through the shoot and into post-production. Once he had that, he was due the next tranche of production money and he'd pay me back. It would be a bridge loan, really, for just a couple of months.

I had a strong feeling that I should refuse politely. My intuition raised a red flag. It was a significant sum. It crossed my mind to question him more, to find out exactly which miscalculation had led him to run out of money in the first place. It even crossed my mind that he'd been an actor once, and therefore was a professional manipulator of other people's emotions. My rational self told me, 'Say no. Or at least, have a formal lending agreement drawn up, witnessed, signed, and copied, before handing over a single naira.'

Yes, you've spotted the outcome. I told him I'd think about it. All torn up with emotion, I awoke the following morning as Saint Chika who would do this good deed and save them all the women and children and friends in need. Still in pyjamas (but now wearing my sparkling new halo), I impulsively wrote him a cheque and a note reminding him of my bank details for repayment, wishing him luck.

He was so excited when he got it. His wife and everybody he could think of called me to thank me. I basked in my saintliness that whole week.

The shoot began on schedule, and he kept in touch with me on its progress.

Soon after, his calls stopped. He must be in post-production, I thought. Editing—it's such a busy time.

The two months went by, and I still didn't hear from him. I decided to call him and find out what was happening. No response. He could see my number, so surely he'd call me back? He didn't.

Are you getting a bad feeling? I was, too.

In the next few months, I called several more times. He never picked up. I had an idea—I borrowed a friend's phone and called from their number. He picked up at once.

'Hi,' I said. 'It's Chik—'

The line went dead.

I was fuming. I had been played for a fool. I hadn't just lost money; I had been treated with disrespect. And then I read that his movie had been released.

I took ten deep breaths and counted backwards from twenty. (Such self-control the girl has!) Grinding my teeth, I sent him a calm, matter-of-fact message to say he still owed the money and would he please pay me, since the debt was overdue.

He rang a few days later.

'Chika?'

'Ah. Long time, no hear from.'

'I got your text. My film isn't out yet. Will you stop harassing me?'

'What? Harassing you? So I'm the bad person? You have a debt to me. PAY IT.'

'What did I just say? As soon as it's out, you'll get your damn money.'

'Don't insult my intelligence. It was released six weeks ago. Fourteenth of June, remember?'

There was a pause. 'Yeah, but I haven't seen a penny from the distributors yet. It's been all outgoings—'

'I'll give you two weeks. Then I'm calling my lawyer.'

I heard nothing, so he got a sharp letter from a firm of solicitors. The legal approach sparked intense activity, but not the kind that repaid my money. Instead, my phone began ringing off the hook. His wife called me, his friends.... His friends were unbelievable: a shower of total airheads with the moral judgement of fleas. I got:

'Hey, why are you getting lawyers involved? Can't a guy just owe money for a few months?' and 'You're upsetting his whole creative life. Just lay off.'

You'd think I'd set out to wreck this genius's career out of malice. As I write, he has not yet paid me a penny, let alone any interest. I have been played for a fool, and he has turned his friends against me.

Do not mix money and emotion. Get all exchanges and agreements involving money in writing. Insist, despite any appeals to friendship or honour. Loans are always properly recorded; otherwise you might as well give the money away. A promise to repay by a given date, including details of any agreed-upon interest or security against the loan, is normal business practice. No sincere person will object to these terms of good business practice. If anyone does, ask yourself why and run the other way.

Get it in writing, or you won't be ABLE to Boss Up.

20

SAVE

You can't just say 'I'm going to be
a millionaire' aloud and hope.

I HAVE ALWAYS WANTED LUXURIES. NOW, I understand that independence and security and friends and good health and travel make me happier than any amount of stuff (as long as I can stay in five-star hotels). But when I was young, so young that my idea of heaven on earth was a Gucci handbag, my mother asked me to make a wish on my sixteenth birthday. I didn't hesitate.

'I want to be a millionaire before I'm 21,' I said.

She laughed. Then she looked searchingly at me. She could see I was serious. I told her I wanted to act in films. She told me I should concentrate on getting into university first. The millions would come later. She was big on education. She had her masters and wanted no less for me.

She had also always encouraged me to save. When I was little, she would give me one naira as a reward for household chores and ask me to show it to her two weeks later. It taught me how to delay gratification. If you learn the secret power of delayed gratification, it makes you capable of finishing your homework before you flop down in front of the TV. It sets you up for a successful and happy life—one in which you work toward goals that truly fulfil you.

So I spoke my birthday wish aloud, wrote it down in my journal, and prayed about it. I already had a plan. I would get into university, and I would make some money (I wasn't sure exactly how). I'd save half of everything I earned until I was a millionaire.

First I started working for my mum, and saving. When I started modelling, I saved some more.

Coming down to earth after months of working and saving, I still wasn't earning a whole lot. So I got real. I said to myself, 'I can't just say 'I'm going to be a millionaire' out loud and hope. I have to work my socks off. I don't come from a rich background.'

True. There were no rich grandparents able to buy me swanky city apartments in Lagos, no long-lost great-aunts about to bequeath me a fortune. Everything our family had was hard-earned by our parents. Like every other family, we'd had brilliant times and some very dark ones, financially. I knew which I preferred.

So I thought I would go to auditions and maybe get picked for a movie.

I acted, I got paid, I saved. I sold shoes, and saved; and I studied for my degree.

When I was coming up to my 21st birthday I went to the bank, and for the first time, I asked the cashier to check my balance. She typed in my name and looked at her computer. It was quite a slow one, and I saw her using the mouse to scroll down the figures. She noted a figure on a piece of paper and pushed it under the grille to me.

I looked at it and thought, *That can't be right.* I asked her to check it again. She gave me a funny look, pressed some buttons on the computer keyboard, crossed the room, and tore off a printout. She came back and pushed it through.

'No, Miss Ike. That's the figure. One million and twenty thousand naira.'

I was so happy. I jumped in the air and screamed, 'I'm a millionaire!' The naira is not worth a lot in other currencies, but hey, I'd achieved my goal! I ran outside, jumped onto the first Okada I saw, and raced home with the breeze against my face. When I showed my parents the balance, they both said they were very proud of me. Which was even better than being a millionaire because Daddy had been absolutely adamant that no daughter of his would ever act in films. He'd thought it was disgraceful. If it hadn't been for my mum, I think he'd have thrown me out on the street. He wasn't a bad man. He was just one of those parents who think they can control their children, choose career paths for them, and bring them up in their own image. No parent can do that.

So I had ambition, and a time-limited goal that I'd already reached, but I knew my ambition still spurred me to greater things. The truth is, I'd prefer to be a dollar millionaire, at least. I have always liked money. I'm perfectly comfortable saying that. I don't care if people are shocked; there is absolutely nothing wrong in wanting to be rich. Certainly it's abhorrent if you'll trample over other people or dump your moral principles just to get money. But if you use wealth to spread a little happiness, to yourself and the world in general, that's surely good?

I couldn't stop saving; I had to do it. Money was my motivation. How to use it? Well, that was a whole other thing.

You can't just say 'I'm going to be a millionaire' aloud and hope.

21

INVEST

Every investment is a risk.
You can lose money as well as make it.

I HADN'T STUDIED AT HARVARD BUSINESS
School yet. That was in the future, when I would start Fancy Nancy
Accessories and learn to think strategically about my business and
try to find out what other people did, and knew, to get the success
they achieved. Before I'd started looking for mentors, before I'd trav-
elled, I still looked to money for independence and handbags. And
dresses. And really good shoes.

But without knowing it, I was investing in myself too because
I loved being alive and I was curious. Everybody should be curious,
like a little kid. If we remain curious, we'll never be bored. In every
spare moment, I read books and watched films about people whose
lives were very different from mine. This broadened my understanding of the world and made me more aware of how unfair it was, and
how often people fell ill.

My father was not very well. Not long ago he'd been able to work and bring up all six of us in comfort, but he'd never paid much attention to his health. I watched his struggle, and I knew I didn't ever want to feel old and sick. I wanted to be as healthy as I could and be full of energy for as long as I could.

Of course, I need a reliable cash flow to live the good life until I am an old woman. I had to think about how to make my million naira provide that healthy, long, and happy life.

What would you do? I'm not saying you shouldn't splurge, take that vacation on your bucket list, or enjoy the gains from your hard work. But financial security is important for long-term mental and physical health. My security about money is the foundation of my whole attitude to life. I want to be able to take a worthwhile risk (like *African Diva*, for instance) without lying awake worrying I might lose everything. Nobody wants to go bankrupt. At the same time, nobody needs thirty pairs of black shoes and twenty white tank tops.

So if you decide to invest your money, don't put your life savings into one thing, because that's not a risk—it's a gamble, and what you're betting is your entire security and way of life. Every investment is a risk. You can lose money as well as make it. Think carefully, read serious news about politics and economics, observe what's going on in the social world around you, and take advice only from someone you trust. And, of course, as with everything else, get it in writing.

I have learned this. It's taken years, but the message is fundamental. I didn't know any of it when I was twenty and deciding to bet my million naira on the word of a friend I trusted. I got super lucky because he could have been a con man. He wasn't. But con men are everywhere, sometimes hiding behind a friendly face, or even a friend's face. What did I know? Pretty much nothing, I admit.

Once I'd celebrated my first million with my family, I set off to spend it. I'd made an appointment to see some designer bags and shoes. Couldn't wait! So I left early, having decided to drop in on Egbon, and tell him my good news. Egbon means 'my elder brother' in Yoruba. He was a friend of the family, older than me, but I used to talk to him, and we could all drop by his office if we wanted to. I'd never been there, and although I knew he was a property developer I had no idea what that meant.

He had a nice office, with a wide desk and a couch and a coffee table. I waited for a while as he was taking a call, surrounded by piles of folded paper. So I came in quietly, sat on the couch, and saw more of these paper stacks on the low table. There wasn't a copy of *Vogue* within reach so I picked one of the folded documents off the top, started to unfold it, and saw inside what looked to be some sort of diagram. I couldn't make it out at all.

Egbon ended his call, made quick notes, and then grinned at me.

'Chika—I'm so glad you've come by. Sorry I'm so busy. Come over and take a chair. What are you looking at?'

I brought the diagram over to his table. I was mystified.

'What is all this? All these drawings?'

'They're plans. Building plans.' I must have looked blank because he added, 'They're the guides you have to follow if you want to build houses somewhere.'

'Oh? Why? Does everybody have those? I thought once you've got cement and blocks you're good to go.'

He laughed so hard that his eyes watered. Then he took another call and said, 'I've got to go out to my site now. I've invested in some new building equipment, and it's just been delivered.'

'Can I come with you? I want to see how it all works. Is it far?'

'If you like. We'll be back in about three hours. You'll have to take care when we're there, though. I don't want you wandering off and falling down a trench.'

I was quite excited. I rang the woman with the shoes and bags to postpone our appointment, and off we went.

In the half hour it took us to drive to the site, I asked questions. Egbon explained about building regulations. I hadn't known there were any. And he explained how expensive house-building was, and that builders had to get bank loans. Loans for building were only given by the bank if it thought your houses would be safe and in a good location, and that they'd sell for plenty of money. The more answers he gave me, the more my interest grew.

I said, 'What if I want to get into construction and get rich and successful like you?'

'How are you going to do that, Chika?'

'I'm going to be a millionaire.'

Obviously, this was the funniest thing he'd ever heard. I took no notice. When he'd stopped giggling, and noticed that I was poker-faced, he said, 'Well, if you invest in property that people want to buy, in a place where they want to buy it, you can't go wrong. You can get really rich if you invest in property.'

We'd entered a small village. When we bumped down the gritty lane that led to his yard, I was super excited. There stood the massive, gleaming machinery that had just arrived. He explained that it was for earth-moving, digging down to make the foundations of a house faster than men with spades could do it. I was looking around, asking him questions about the tiles and piping I could see stacked up around me. When he finished checking over the equipment, we drove out of the yard to go to a site a few miles away, nearer to the city.

The first thing I saw was a cement mixer. Not that I knew that was what the machine was called. All I saw was a big round noisy sort of dish with men pouring sand, pebbles, and water into it. The machine noisily ground the stones into cement dust and mixed the whole lot together to make concrete. There was no pump. Instead the mix flowed sluggishly out along a trough to where a team of topless labourers collected buckets of heavy, grey concrete and jogged off to where other men were building a house. Everything was done at jogging pace so that the concrete wouldn't have time to set before it was poured. It was hot, sweaty, and dangerous work, I was thinking, when Egbon appeared in front of me wearing boots and a helmet. He had an armful of the same equipment for me.

'I'm going onto the site. If you want to come with me, you'll have to wear these.'

My eyebrows shot up.

'Building sites can be dangerous, and it's the law.'

'Okay, I'm coming.'

I was fumbling with the chinstrap of my helmet when my phone rang and I had to take it off again. It was the woman I was supposed to buy the shoes and bags from. I told her I'd like to make it tomorrow instead, and kept the call short. I was totally engaged by everything I was learning on the site, and wearing my new headgear and footwear—which was super hot, and not in a fashionable way—I followed Egbon into the building.

Within minutes he'd found some mistake or other and had begun a shouting match with his engineer. I'd never seen him so angry before. The louder they yelled, the more I began to regret this experience and skipping what I was born to do (i.e., find something by Prada). Glumly I guessed he'd be in a filthy mood after this. I couldn't face any transferred aggression as I was sticky with perspiration and my black pants looked as if I'd rolled in dust.

When the argument was over, the rest of the building had been inspected, and Egbon was calm again, he told me his next call would be to a client who wanted to buy some hectares of land from him in Epe. He'd give me a lift back into Lagos if I wanted, but I was welcome to come with him instead.

Epe is near the sea, about an hour and a half's drive from where we were, and I had nothing better to do so I said I'd like to come. Out on the open road, with the aircon cooling me down, I felt calm and happy and inspired.

'Why does this man want to buy the hectares?'

'He'll build on it and sell houses, I think. There's always demand from tourists over there, so people buy houses and rent them out.'

'Will he make a lot of money out of it?'

'Well, he has a good chance. It's a great site. But he'll get it at a discount because it's right on the edge of Epe, so the services will have to be installed across virgin land.'

'Services?'

'Electricity and water. Sewage pipes. You have to pay the city. Expensive.'

We got to the site, and the potential buyer was already waiting for us. We were all introduced, and then the two men started pacing out the boundaries of the plots, talking about millions of naira and people I didn't know, and my shoes were getting filthy, so after about five minutes I snuck back to the car and put the aircon on. I'd wanted to look, and I'd looked. This was the bush, as far as I was concerned. I imagined living here with shops and streets and cinemas was a distant dream.

Egbon came back and got behind the wheel with a smile on his face. We set off back to Lagos through whole flocks of swerving, tooting Okadas.

'You look very pleased,' I said.

'Yes. He seems like a serious buyer.'

'I want to buy some land.'

He grinned. 'You'll need to be rich.'

'I'm rich already. I saved up.'

'You serious?'

'Yes. I told you.'

'So how much have you saved up?'

'I'm a millionaire.'

'Now come on, Chika.'

'I am.'

'Well, you never know—one day.'

He probably thought I was really odd. But he politely changed the subject, and we talked about my family and his all the way back. But that night, I couldn't go to sleep. I kept thinking about everything that I'd seen that day and the millions I'd heard them discussing.

So next day, I called him quite early and arranged to drop by again.

In his office, I told him how much I'd been gripped by what I'd seen and heard the previous day. Then I said, 'I really do want to buy some land.'

'With what, Chika?'

'I'm a millionaire, I told you. I saved up.'

'How much have you saved up?'

'A million naira, of course. And I don't want land in the bush. I want it in a developed area.'

He laughed. 'I like your style, Chika. But land where you want it costs far more than that. I'll give you some advice. It's a great thing to have saved so much and to want to invest it, but for the next few years just put all your savings in a fixed deposit account, so that the interest compounds. In any case, you're too young to sign a contract. You have to be 21.'

'I'll be old enough next month. And you said yourself, the price of land is rising.'

'Yes, but a million will only buy you a tiny strip out in the bush. I can sell you one of those if you want. But there's nothing out there.'

I was so disappointed. He told me not to be, and I went to see the shoe lady. My heart wasn't in it, though, and I didn't spend much.

The next day Egbon called me.

'I have been thinking. You were lucky for me the other day. I don't want to discourage you. I'm really impressed that you're even thinking of doing this when most girls your age are thinking of shoes and handbags.'

As if!

'There is something you can possibly invest in. Come with me to Ajah this morning.'

I was so excited. I drove there with him. It's not far from the Lagoon, and the streets were not paved, but people were living there and I saw a lot of construction sites. We drove along a bumpy road towards thick bush and swamp. When we could go no farther, he parked and we got out.

'See that palm tree?'

'Yes.'

'Well, I own seven plots between there and that end of the road. I'll sell one of them to you.'

'How much do you want for it?'

'Three million. But you brought me luck yesterday, so I'll sell it to you for two and you can pay me back whenever.'

'Thank you. But I want two plots.'

'Listen, I'm trying to encourage you, Chika, but that's six million naira!'

'Well, four, with the discount.'

'Come on! Let's say I do let you have two plots for four million, you've only got a million, so how will you pay me back?'

I said, 'I'll pay you one million now. I'll give you another million in one year, and the other two million as soon as I've got the money.'

Egbon stared at me thoughtfully for a while. Then he stretched out his hand. 'It's a deal.' I beamed as I shook his hand.

'I'm so excited! I just sealed my first real estate deal.

'Your parents should be proud of you.'

'Thank you!' I couldn't stop grinning. By the time my birthday came, I'd had the contract from him and it was with my lawyer for approval. Soon afterwards, I signed. I've gone on since then to invest in more land and to develop property on it. Fame can be short-lived, handbags go out of fashion, but if you save and invest while you're young, all kinds of possibilities will open up. Be ready to take advantage of them.

Every investment is a risk. You can lose money as well as make it.

22

STEP
BACK

Take a long view.
Then take a decision.

I KNOW EXACTLY HOW I CAME TO RECOGNISE the value of focus. I was running Fancy Nancy Accessories, and a Nollywood career. I was dabbling in so many new businesses. What would take off? I didn't know which one to think about next. There were so many new ideas, new entrants to the industry. Who was coming in out of passion, and who was just working for the money?

I was making decisions from day to day, fighting fires all over the place, seeing everything from the point of view of now. I needed to take a step back and take a long view. So I took three months out for R&R. The rest part was over in a few days. The recovery meant taking stock.

I wrote down all my issues and conflicts, and for what it's worth, here's the list:

What are the opportunities I have?

What is my long-term plan?

Who am I really working for? Am I acting in films, or advertisements?

How do I construct my own niche, my own brand?

I tried to look at all these questions and identify why I was currently confused. I made another list.

My problems were:

Lack of focus (I was trying to do too many things at once).

Being too easily distracted (I'd sprint away with a concept but start another one before I'd properly concentrated on the first).

In three months, I had a whole list of new ideas. But ideas are the easy part. I needed to winnow down the list. I sifted through, looked at each of them, placed them in order of preference. To do that I had to decide what I really wanted—to make a lot of money or to just be an actress; to be a TV star or a retailer with a chain of shops; to help a lot more children or to become a property developer.

I decided that yes, I was happy to keep my property development projects and retail accessories growing because they interested me and made money, much of which I would donate to my charitable foundation. But more than anything, I wanted to present a reality TV show. That was where I had to focus.

That three-month rest was one of the most productive times in my life. At the end of it, I had refined and polished the concept of *African Diva*.

Take a long view. Then take a decision.

23

ACT
INNOCENT

Use assertiveness with care. It can
have unwanted side effects.

SOMETIMES IT'S GOOD TO CONCEAL WHAT you know. Acting wise all the time can cause problems. Most people, especially your boss or a superior, don't want you to be always the smart one. They don't necessarily want your strong, well-founded opinion before they've asked for it. They'll feel less threatened if you seem just a little uncertain of your ground. Assert yourself, but don't try too hard. I was once talking to an investor in a project I was involved in. I talked knowledgeably, because I wanted him to know that I had grasped the financial and fiscal implications of his decision. But I saw he was uneasy, almost intimidated—maybe thinking that if we went into business, I might outsmart him. He was supposed to be bringing money to the table; I was trying to show him I was competent. All I did was scare him off.

Is the message therefore, 'Don't be too clever for your own good? Conflict Avoidance for Girls?' Of course not. I am absolutely not advocating that you make concessions to loudmouths. You have to be assertive, or others will always hold the floor in meetings and your views will be dismissed or—and this is worse—ignored when you put them forward, but re-framed two minutes later and presented as someone else's (but I just SAID that! Grrrr).

It's just that you mustn't go too far. (Example: 'Leave me to deal with international licensing, John. Don't you bother your pretty little head about it.')

I am a pragmatist, and there's more than one way to get where you're going. I prefer the way where both sides win.

You know about mansplaining—when a man explains in a patronising tone something you already know. It's infuriating. But do start the business relationship on an unthreatening note. Exploit the fact that everybody likes to be asked about whatever it is they're most interested in. Even more than that, they like to be asked simple questions, because they can give simple answers.

Therefore, do ask, 'Why doesn't a boat sink?'

Don't ask, 'Can you explain the effect of buoyancy force versus gravitational pull?'

You can move imperceptibly to the complexities that interest you when they've given you the Mickey-Mouse version.

Take care, though. 'Why is the sky blue?' is a question raised by most two-year-olds. A question too simple risks making us look ignorant. If we haven't got superfast broadband immediately on hand, we'll probably stumble to find an accurate response.

If you, in your turn, are questioned, never claim to know the answer if you don't. Admit that you don't, but promise to do your best to find out.

Use assertiveness with care. It can have unwanted side effects.

24

JUST
DO
IT

Do it tired, do it scared, do
it confused—just do it!

THE REASON WHY SO MANY IDEAS DON'T come to anything is that we overthink. Every possible aspect is picked up, turned around, looked at from a million angles. What if it breaks? What if it won't work? What if nobody likes it?

Some people can't even decide what they want for dinner because they overthink, prevaricate, dither, and hesitate until the dinner is in the dog. Opportunity lost.

Here is how not to waste a whole day choosing from a thousand selfies for your Instagram page. It is Chika's Two-minute Instagram Method (patent pending):

- Set a stopwatch on your phone for 60 seconds.

- Choose three selfies before the 60 seconds are up.

- Now set the stopwatch for 30 seconds.

- Time's up! You've chosen The One. Put it on Instagram.

- Do it tired, do it scared, do it confused—just do the damn thing.

Caution has caused too many business partnerships to die before they start. You've both got to be bubbling with enthusiasm and willing to work all hours. Above all, you both have to take a risk. If one of you is risk-averse, you'll inevitably fall out, leaving two disappointed people.

I have learned over the years to have a bright idea and just get on it. To Boss Up, in fact.

I wasn't born this way. I was born cautious. I'd been selling shoes and bags to friends for years, and I wanted to set up my own business, Fancy Nancy Accessories… one day.

One day arrived. It always does, but you have to look out for it and seize it when it comes—and I didn't know that. One day a friend told me about a shop in Abuja that was up for rent. I didn't have the money. I knew how to market, knew about shoes and bags, knew I had a clientele, but I didn't take action.

Instead I sat on a giant mushroom, looking at the stars, smoking an imaginary hookah pipe and pondering the meaning of life. Or something. I don't know what I did, but the shop remained empty. Whole empty days went past, days when I could have been making money. Other retailers started to show an interest.

Another friend could bear it no longer. He offered me a loan if I'd take the shop and open it up. I accepted, opened Fancy Nancy, and paid him back in three months.

Just do it. Delay means missed opportunities and lost money. That was a lesson for me.

Do it
TIRED
Do it
SCARED
Do it
CONFUSED
Just
DO IT!

25

DISCRETION

Treat your ideas like precious rubies
because they are just as valuable.

IN BUSINESS, DISCRETION IS ABSOLUTELY KEY.
You may otherwise face dishonesty, negativity, or lack of momentum.

First, dishonesty. People may steal your ideas, or undermine them by telling someone else who then steals them. If you have a really bright idea, it has value to someone who can raise the money to make the widget, or the TV show, or the new chain-free bicycle. As it's the product of your creativity, you should not put it out in the world until you have secured a patent, or the intellectual property rights and the copyright, in writing.

There is no copyright for ideas, but you can own copyright in a fully developed concept. So once you'd developed the idea, put it onto paper in as much detail as you can, seal it up, ask your bank to keep it, and get a dated receipt (there may be a small fee for this, as there is if you deposit it with a lawyer). Alternatively, you can send the paperwork to yourself and keep the envelope unopened, in a safe place. (The postmark gives the date, and the contents will reveal that you did originate the idea when you said you did.) You can't rely on having copyright in a developed concept until you have somehow made a record of it—until then, it's an idea and you can't copyright that. And you can't get an official registration or patent for a product until you've supplied even more detail: precise measurements, suggested materials, and properly drawn plans, for instance, showing how it will work.

So don't blab. Treat your ideas like precious rubies because they can be just as valuable. Keep them safe.

Suppose I'm Miuccia Prada. She's a billionaire, and a class act. She and her team work in Milan designing bags that sell for between $1,500 and $5,000. The precise specification for each design is registered. Every possible measurement of every tiny constituent part of the bag, and the materials it's made of, plus photos and measurements of the prototype, are recorded and logged with the appropriate government office as her design. Her studio will also retain notes from the design meetings and records of payment to suppliers. So if a manufacturer sells knock-off copies that are superficially identical, they can easily be shown to have stolen Prada's design and undermined her reputation by adding her name to rubbish. In other words, cheating her of an income. If they do it on a considerable scale, her lawyers will take them to court where they will prove that the design is hers using all the documentation they so carefully kept. The knock-off makers will have to pay a painful amount; it may put them out of business.

Do you think Miuccia Prada would show the world her designs before they're launched? Treat your ideas with the same care and concern.

Second, beware of negativity. It's understandable. In most fields of endeavour, you know where to go for backing: people who've done it before. If you are a complete unknown, and you've got a film script or the manuscript of a novel, you go to a producer or agent or publisher. If you're unknown with a portfolio of dress designs, you approach a design house or a big manufacturer. These industry people see zillions of scripts and manuscripts and portfolios, and they know that out of twenty thousand unsolicited applications every year they'll probably choose two. At most.

Don't expect to be met with open arms. They won't roll out the welcome mat for you. It's really, really hard to get started if you are an unknown quantity, and it's absolutely impossible if your idea is half-baked. It's foolish to put anything out there until it's up and running or at any rate ready to launch. You will need to be certain of its excellence before people will take it seriously. Just make sure you protect your rights, listen carefully to feedback on your perfect concept from the people who are turning you down, and be prepared to adjust it and improve it and try again and again, with increasing confidence rather than increasing despair, until you succeed.

Third, an obstacle is a failure of momentum. If you describe your ideas vividly to the world at an early stage, they'll probably falter and hiccup to a stop, and become lost to oblivion, because you'll frighten yourself with the amount of work left to do. Creative ideas don't emerge fully formed. When I want to start a new business and if I talk about a half-formed concept, ask about its appeal to others, or even think aloud about it, somehow it never ultimately works out. It flops before it starts.

Much better to give it time. Go to bed with possibilities buzzing and wake up with those that are realisable. Write them down. Make notes or a mind-map. Assemble them to completion. Make the concept perfectly real in your mind. Carry on adding to it and adjusting it until it's perfect. Don't talk about it. Ideas are like mushrooms. They need an undisturbed place to grow in.

Treat your ideas like precious rubies because they are just as valuable.

26

WORK SMART

Being busy isn't the same
as being productive.

IT'S GOOD TO WORK HARD, RIGHT? OF COURSE
it is. But look around, and you'll see a lot of people hard at work who
never seem to achieve much.

Being busy isn't the same as being productive. The formula is:

Hard work + Smart work = Success

Smart work is directed. It is planned in advance. It is doing
whatever it takes to achieve your goal and exceed it. It means getting
organised short-term in pursuit of a long-term aim.

You're aiming for a distant goal, so don't set off without a route
map. Imagine driving from Lagos to Cape Town. By road, it's at least
four and a half thousand miles. You work out the best route, which
crosses quite a few borders, and you find out where you can stay
and how far you intend to drive between overnight stops. You pre-
pare yourself with passport and visas, currency, new spare tyre, extra

petrol and water... there's a lot to do. You get on the internet and check to see whether there are places you really should avoid driving through and where you can stay overnight. If you plan properly, you will make it and the journey may even be pleasant.

If you set off without a map, without even a mosquito net or a spare jerry can or enough money, you'll probably end up turning back at the first border.

Same goes for your working life. Having no direction, being stuck in a job because it's just about bearable and it's easy, is futile. Boss Up to your future. Think through your plans. Find out how other people have raised themselves from mediocrity. Have a long-term aim in mind (for instance, buying your own small but delightful island in the Seychelles) and travel towards it in short-term steps, as if you were climbing up a ladder. Every day, you will work towards the next step. Each promotion you achieve, every naira you save and invest, will take you closer to your distant goal. From one year to the next, you will make progress, and you will measure it.

Organisation is everything. Busy people are disciplined. Their time is allocated in advance, and their time is also prioritised. The most important things get the most time. Time management isn't just a matter of writing a list of things to do today, but of trying to find the best way to spend today. Will you lie awake tonight if you haven't bought a lipstick? Probably not. Will you regret losing a client because you forgot a meeting? Probably.

My to-do list relaxes me because I can tick off nearly all of it every night. (One of the best feelings in the world!) I factor in my rest intervals, and I find myself accomplishing much, much more. People say, 'If you want something done, ask a busy person.' Armed with a schedule, if you can fit in an unexpected task, you'll know whether you have time or if you really don't. So you won't over-promise and (in the end) under-deliver, which makes everybody feel bad, and hurts you more than anyone else in the long run. Better to send an apologetic no in the first place.

The point is to spend as much time as possible with an easy, uncluttered mind, avoiding stress-points such as what to wear. You remember how Cinderella's fairy godmother said, 'Cinders, you SHALL go to the Ball!' Then she waved her wand and Whizz! There stood Cinderella with her hair in an updo, eyelashes like silky black brushes, her nails little pink shells, and her vast skirts all a-twinkle? Hah! Girls, this is but a dream, a fantasy. The nails alone would take an hour.

If you want to look your best, avoid a mad rush in the mornings. Every night, allocate ten minutes to deciding what to wear the following day. Check that it's actually there and not in the wash or lacking a button, and then go to sleep. When you wake up and the clock is ticking, you won't have to waste time finding the right thing to wear.

And if you possibly can, have a regular clear-out. The enemy of organisation is paperwork you will never require again, clothes you always think you'll wear again but won't, and fabulous boots that feel like a lobster has seized your toe. Bin it or donate it, but unclutter your life.

For six years I failed to write the book that I dreamed of writing. It was at the top of my vision list for so long that most days, I didn't even see it. It was like the name of the newspaper—you read everything else but the banner at the top. In that time, though, I had taken many steps towards other personal goals, and I'd scheduled them in to my diary every day, and they all worked out. We have to prioritise, and when it came down to it, I was over-promising to myself. This book should have been noted as a low priority in 2010 because I wasn't yet ready to write it. In 2017, I was ready, and it finally belonged at the top of the list.

You probably know lots of busy non-planners who are forever standing about looking important or dashing down a corridor. They're working. It's just that they're working at a low, slow rate (even though they may look rushed) because they lack focus. They look something up on the internet, and half an hour later they're still there, following clickbait to pictures of celebrities before and after plastic surgery, or drinking at lunchtime and falling asleep for an hour mid-afternoon, or arguing about football as they hang out around the watercooler. There are all kinds of ways to be unproductive, and they add up to wasted years.

When you see that your high rate of productivity has made you extra valuable to your clients or employers, don't forget to increase your fee, or ask for a raise. If you can't get it, and can't see another employer or client on the horizon, then try to invest in your value on the labour market. Make your time more valuable than ever by training in some new skill within your field.

Being busy isn't the same as being productive.

27

KNOW YOUR BUSINESS

If you set up multiple income streams,
Boss Up. Don't ever neglect them.

'I WANT TO BE AN ACTRESS.'

A lot of people want to be famous, so they decide to be actors.
They don't like to study, or do research. They don't like to hone the
craft. They don't even know their craft. So if somebody says to me
that they want to be an actor, I have to ask:

- Have you studied acting?

- Do you know what it's about?

- Have you ever researched a character?

- Do you know how to handle fame?

- Or money?

- Do you want to be famous forever, or for five minutes?

I didn't go to drama school. When I started, I didn't study theatre arts. I was naturally good at it, but that is never enough. Fortunately for me, I worked with good people and learned as much as I could from them. Acting requires more than simply inventing a character's walk, the way they talk, their facial expressions. And there's a lot of work out there, beyond Nollywood and beyond film, too. So I took myself off to acting school in Los Angeles for six months. I learned a lot, and came back ready to tackle new challenges.

Some jobs have a short shelf-life. Careers in sport, modelling, or pop music really can be over and done in ten years. There are exceptions. A few famous models are still working in their seventies, and others, like Elle MacPherson, have built businesses thanks to their fame. Many sports people have gone on to management, top-level coaching, or broadcasting. There are pop stars who have quit while they're ahead and gone on to succeed in other careers.

However, the vast majority of people who are famous in their twenties either live off that ancient fame for the rest of their lives, or—if they didn't earn that much despite the fame—find themselves, at thirty, looking around for another job in a market where everyone else their age has more relevant experience.

I mention all this because there are people in Nollywood who don't expect to get work after their looks have faded. Odd, really, since stories have older characters too, but… many young stars sensibly decide to back some kind of business while they're big earners, and let another competent person build it up. Then, when hard times come, they will at least have a good income.

They think.

But, oh, dear. Most un-involved investors are happy as long as everything ticks over. Unfortunately, business isn't like that; to be successful, it has to grow. So the person who has the most to lose if the business fails to thrive must be vigilant. If you're going to put money into an agency, or a restaurant, or an interior design company, you need to know what's going on in the business on a daily basis. Avoid interfering, because micromanaging by someone who isn't working directly in the enterprise is guaranteed to make staff resentful. I don't suggest you micro-manage.

But there are taxes, there are wages, there are profit margins to be assessed, and if running this business were your job you'd have to know the figures for yesterday's takings every day at 8 am; does the person in charge know that? Your strategy. Your interest rate. Who's really in control? Your accountant is an advisor, not a managing director. If you are lending your name and your money to this business, you need to be able to benchmark your marketing team's performance against others.

You are right to set up multiple income streams, as long as you don't neglect them. Neglect breeds problems; they multiply when out of sight and out of mind. Many showbiz stars have been poorly served, or even swindled, by people they employ. Keep on top of your investment. There's little point in opening a fabulous restaurant that goes broke and takes your pension with it.

BOSS UP! TO DO LIST

List all the business mistakes you've made in the past and why you made them.

List five types of business you'd love to venture into.

Prioritize them. Which are the three that you are more passionate about? Which comes first of the bunch, and why?

Do you have anyone around you or within your reach in that line of business that can be a mentor to you?

List five people you can write to or ask to support your business.

Write a letter to your future self about what you want to achieve, with deadlines. Mark your calendar or set a reminder on your mobile phone to open the letter a year after you write it.

If you
set up
multiple
income
streams,
Boss Up.
Don't ever
neglect them.

PART 4

SOCIETY

'Surround yourself only with people
who are going to take you higher.'

—Oprah Winfrey

28

DEVELOP RHINO SKIN

'Sticks and stones may break my
bones, but words can never hurt me.'

THE RHINOCEROS, A MAGNIFICENT BEAST, HAS
hide that can be up to five centimetres thick. *Rhino* is a byword for
toughness; which is sad, because rhinos are peace-loving, short-
sighted vegetarians who have been almost wiped off the face of
the earth by poachers with guns. Yes, their skin is thick, but it can
be penetrated by a bullet, which is largely why they're threatened
with extinction.

So if you are insulted online, or humiliated, or hated, remember
the old saying: 'Sticks and stones may break my bones, but words can
never hurt me.'

You are not being shot at like a defenceless rhino. You're some
muppet's hate object for the day, but so what? Boss Up. Words can't
hurt you. If you let them get under your skin, the haters have won.

Develop rhino skin. And if you feel like dumping your Facebook account, you're in good company. Meghan Markle, due in May 2018 to become the first mixed-race member of the British Royal Family (therefore probably Princess Henry of Wales and also a Duchess), closed down all her social media early in the year.

Mark Zuckerberg won't miss you, either. Promise.

'Sticks
and stones
may break
my bones,
but words
can never
hurt me.'

29

PRIVACY

Don't over-share.

PRIVACY IS AS IMPORTANT IN DAILY LIFE AS discretion is in business. Revealing a little of yourself is enough. Don't over-share what's good in your life, what you're about, what you're doing, who helped you, what happened—how you got this, how you got that—because if you're not careful, you'll provide ammunition for the spiteful. Some people will smile and seem to be your friend, but they'll be jealous. They'll have a scornful voice inside, grumbling, 'Why's she so great? Why are all these things going well for her?'

While I was first married I used to tell my BFF how wonderful and how considerate my husband was. (I had mentally excused his nasty moods to make myself feel better.) I told her how understanding he was when he saw me working, how relaxing it was to spend an evening with him.

I was thought I was saying was, 'Hey, I'm so lucky that I fell in love with this guy!' What she heard was, 'Hey, look at me. Poor you, by comparison.' She was single, and more sensitive about that than I realised.

During my exams I found a place to stay close to the university, so that I could study quietly but get to the exam hall fast. My neighbour from home dropped by to see me one day. She kept casually mentioning my best friend. Then—

'That girl,' she said, 'is sleeping with your husband.'

I was shocked. 'Why would you say that? She's not like that. She's always been there for me. She's my best friend!'

I was thinking, *How could this woman imagine such a thing?* Yes, a tiny seed of doubt was sown, but I just knew she had to be lying. (It's called blaming the messenger.)

She insisted. 'I looked out of the window, and I could see them making out in your apartment.'

I refused to believe her. But she did not budge from her version of the truth. I didn't want to seem so dismissive, so I calmed down and asked her questions. I couldn't deny it any longer. I could tell she was telling the truth.

I called my best friend. She was all indignation. Said it was a wicked lie. I wanted to believe her, but I didn't. A month later, after I'd had a big showdown with my husband, she called me and admitted it and apologised. I felt betrayed.

What I regretted most was everything I'd told her about my marriage. I'd wanted her to be happy for me. But I had been rubbing salt into a wound I didn't even know she had. And I'll never know whether she really desired my husband or whether she went with him just to spite me. Probably a bit of both.

So don't sing your good fortune from the mountaintop... not even to your best friends, because people will inevitably compare your life with theirs and unless they're secure and happy, they may resent you.

Even more important, don't tell them about your failures. If you tell a funny story against yourself, someone will repeat it with a sneer and a nasty spin. There's always at least one person who's glad of any excuse to ignore your successes, amplify your failures, and direct every kind of scorn at you from behind your back. Social media multiplies all of this by ten.

Don't over-share

30

STOP THE GOSSIP

'No comment' is good.
Silence is better.

GOSSIP CAN BE THE CONVERSATIONAL EQUIV-
alent of ice cream: delicious, but better avoided. If it's about a
celebrity—somebody you don't know, but just see on TV and the
internet—it's fun, it's fascinating, it seems harmless, and it's a socia-
ble link with other people who are just as interested. You may
unknowingly be repeating stonking lies about the star's love life.
Even so, you're probably doing him or her a favour because if you
gossip about people, you give them power by raising their profile.
Most film actors have been linked to somebody they hardly know,
online or in the press. They just shrug and say, 'No publicity is bad
publicity' and move on. They know that their real friends know it's
a lie. They also know that this imaginary affair they're having will
register their name in the public consciousness. And that's valuable;

the better known they are, the bigger the audience they'll attract and the bigger the fee they'll command.

When I started to make a name for myself, I didn't understand this. The first time I was linked to somebody was after I became divorced. I hadn't even met the man, and I took it personally, as if My Honour Had Been Impugned (Tttt!) by the journalist or blogger who dreamed up the story. I was genuinely upset. Fabricated gossip of that kind can't last. It demands a regular stream of real-life photo opportunities. (Chika and Mr. X out clubbing. Chika and Mr. X fly in from Cape Town.) With no photo opportunities, there is no story. Any rumours will quickly evaporate.

Nowadays I've Bossed Up. I think that if lies about actors having affairs are some sad person's preferred reading, hey, nobody died.

Gossip about private individuals is different. Unless they have money, they can't fly out of the country to get away, they can't threaten legal action, they can't hire people to put out their point of view in mass media. And online gossip is the worst. In a little community, if somebody starts talking about an affair that Mrs. Y and Mr. X may or may not be having, the two people can't strike back without feeding the whole story. Even if they ignore it and it dies down, mud will stick and their lives might never be the same again.

That could happen to somebody you know. 'No comment' is good, but silence is better. Avoid gossip.

'No comment'
is good.
Silence is
better.

31

TAKE A STAND

'If you stand for nothing,
you fall for everything.'

YOU MUST HAVE GUIDING PRINCIPLES.

What I hate most is injustice and bullying. It's ever-present, but good people can choose to defend the victim.

Maybe you first saw bullying in the schoolyard. Bullies are really scared of being considered a weak person, which is why they like to sneer and mock at kids who are poor or frail or in some other way different. Bullies gain an advantage when they do this, because other children join in out of fear. The victim, the one who's different, needs a defender. It's hard, but sticking up for your principles is right.

You may think you've never seen injustice or theft or bullying. But things happen out of the blue; you've got to have your principles at the ready, and Boss Up to them.

I'll give you a simple example. Suppose you see an older woman jump in front of girl who was standing at the front of the queue for a train ticket. The girl politely says, 'Excuse me. This is a queue. It's my turn.' The woman turns away from the booking clerk and yells a stream of abuse at the poor girl.

This happened in front of me, and I said respectfully to the older woman, 'Please leave her alone. We all have to take our turn. You can be polite.' I didn't shout. I didn't tell her what I thought of her. I didn't demean her in any way. I somehow knew that to make her listen, I had to speak with authority. So in an undertone I said, 'I think if you apologise and go to the back of the queue, she won't take it any further.'

That's what she did. I hadn't made a fool of her, or it might have been more difficult. But I look back on situations like that, and I'm ashamed of other situations where I didn't intervene; I dithered, thought I'd better not interfere, wondered if I should, and so on. If you're clear about what's happening and what you stand for, take action.

'If you
stand for
nothing,
you fall for
everything.'

32

LOOK DOWN THE MOUNTAIN

The person who gives what they can is the person who gives from the heart.

SUCCESS ISN'T MEASURED BY MONEY OR POS-sessions. It's measured by the people who benefit from what you can give, whether that's laughter, love, or their first meal in a week.

People who spend their lives climbing financially and socially, getting richer, meeting people who are even more stupendously wealthy and forever trying to become richer still—and those are the world's billionaires—often forget to look down the mountain. Know what? It's easy to slip and fall. A billionaire on his mountain-top may become ill from an incurable disease, and all the money in the world will not save him. In that situation, he may envy the child in rags on the street.

Familiarity breeds invisibility. Beggars are always there, so we don't see them.

It doesn't matter how much or how little you have. If you go through life without noticing the poor, the maimed, the sick, the strays, if you never try to help them, you're not properly alive to your own beautiful life. You have to look back down the mountain to appreciate how lucky you are. I was brought up by a mother who taught us to set aside money for good causes. If you have no money, you may have time, or intellectual resources, or physical strength. You can give talks, clean the home of a disabled person, inspire children to learn, or find sponsors and run a race for charity. The person who gives from the heart is someone who gives what she can.

Where I grew up, lots of kids had only the clothes they stood up in and no money for school. Mum donated food, schoolbags, Bibles, pencils, our outgrown clothes. She organised a Christmas party for children and handed out Christmas parcels for old people. When I was at university, and saw that street kids were still around, still neglected, I decided to set up a foundation one day to help them. The one day came, and CIF, the Chika Ike Foundation, exists. It's great to see kids getting maths sets and notebooks and qualifying for scholarships; I love our annual party. And I talk to kids all over Nigeria about the importance of education. If you help to educate a boy or girl, you help them climb out of poverty into a more aspirational mind-set. Not only that, the children you help will be able to one day show their own children a world they never had.

You are fortunate in so many ways. Please give back.

The person who gives what they can is the person who gives from the heart.

BOSS UP! TO DO LIST

Have you ever given back to your society? List what you have done and what you have to give (time, money, goods, etc.).

What can you do to give back more?

Do you let people's opinion about you weigh you down? Why?

What can you do that will help you get out of such a mood when it arises (music, self-assurance, uplifting words or prayers, etc.)?

Have you called a long-time friend, relative, or classmate to tell them thanks for something they did that helped you? Why?

PART 5

❙ ❙ ❙ ❙ ❙ ❙ ❙ ❙ ❙ ❙

FAMILY AND RELATIONSHIPS

'People keep talking about the "normal" family, but I don't think it exists.'

—Anonymous

33

LETTING GO

Walk away from any relationship
that damages your self-esteem.

I TOOK THE BEATINGS FOR FIVE YEARS AFTER
my wedding day. Leaving an abuser means admitting that you've
been co-dependent. You're not running away, but letting go of a person who doesn't love you after all. You're letting go of a fantasy, to
step back into your real life where happiness is possible.

One time while I was still married, probably in the first year, I
took my little dog and left to spend the night in a hotel. But I went
back the next day. I was scared to turn away from the perfect image
I'd been trying to create. Leaving meant admitting: This man is never
going to change. He doesn't even like me.

At the slightest provocation or none, he'd hit me. My sister vis-
ited one day, and when I made some harmless remark he looked
angry and only just stopped himself from landing a blow. I linched.

My sister looked shocked. Into the ensuing silence she said, 'Did you almost hit Chika then?'

He walked out. I think I was crying. My sister called my mum. My mum called me. I admitted that there were difficulties, but it would be okay.

'Are you crazy, Chika? This has been going on for five years and you haven't told me until now? Why not?'

'Well, I thought he'd change. He will... he does try. Really, it doesn't happen every day.'

'How often does it happen, then?'

'Mommy, there's no point. It's getting better. It'll be fine. Let's not rock the boat.'

'Chika, I am your mother. Listen to me. It will not get better. Abusive relationships only get worse.'

'No, it'll all be fine.'

I was so confused. I didn't want to be single. I liked being part of a couple—the public part of it. Behind closed doors, I was living in fear. Not long afterwards, we had another disagreement, and he ordered me to SHUT UP.

So I did. He kept talking and striding around the living room and I said nothing.

'Say something! I'm talking to you.'

I looked at my hands.

'Chika, TALK.'

'You told me to shut up. So I have. I don't want to provoke you.'

'OH, so it's all my fault now. I'm the one who gets angry. I'm the mad person. Come on—talk.'

'I don't know what to say. I'm too scared.'

'You're scared of me. Am I the devil? Oh, it's because you think you are beautiful. Oh, what a superstar, Oh, what a perfect wife... I will destroy you today.'

He picked up a glass jug and hurled it at me, hard. I dodged, and it shattered against the wall. There was glass everywhere.

That would have been my face if I had not ducked in time. This man can kill me.

I looked at the broken jug and the shards gleaming on the floor, and I knew what to do. I'd Boss Up, whatever it took. I would get out while there was still time.

You have to walk away from any relationship that damages your self-esteem. It might be your last chance. Do it now. Before it gets worse.

The future is bright.

Walk away from any relationship that damages your self-esteem.

34

KNOW YOUR WORTH

If you feel undervalued, by
changing the pattern of
transactions between you, you
may restore the power balance.

I'D HAD AN AWFUL MARRIAGE AND A PAINFUL
divorce. I'd been needy, and I still hadn't gotten over the sadness of
my loss, even if it was the loss of a fantasy I worked so hard to create. I needed self-discipline. I needed to be the sort of person who
doesn't get infatuated by the next man who comes along spinning
promises and dreams that won't come true.

I worked out how to do it. I'm quite pleased with myself for
doing this, although the whole method involves far more detail than
I can share in this book. I'll tell you the short version. First of all, let
me set the stage. I had a post-divorce boyfriend. I was in love again.

And guess what? I was making pretty much the same mistakes
I'd made when I met the first husband. I would say, 'You're late, where
have you been?' or 'Why didn't you call sooner? Don't you love me

anymore?' I would call him whenever I felt like it, wanting to hear his voice. It was all about me.

The new boyfriend, of course, didn't see it that way. To him, our relationship wasn't all about me. He perceived my words and attention as whining and nagging. It seemed to him that I was trying to own him and smother him. So he switched off. He ignored the dog-whistle and trotted on his own sweet way, with a life that increasingly diverged from mine.

I could understand that because I, too, prefer independence. One day, for the umpteenth time he didn't return my call. That was the day I said to myself, 'Chika, don't nag and don't call. You are wasting your breath and your energy. Save it for your children.'

I didn't call him. A day passed. And another and another. On the fifth day, he called me. 'Are you all right? Why didn't you call? What's the problem?'

See what I did there? Keep quiet, and you will have results. Change the routine of the transactions between you. Alterations of any kind helps you get your power back. From then on, if he came back late or didn't call, I disciplined myself. I didn't even mention it.

There is a classic book about this. It's been in print since the early 1960s and it's still selling. Millions of people have read it. It's called *Games People Play,* and it's quite funny, but full of insight. Eric Berne, who wrote it, popularised a whole school of psychology about what we're really saying when we talk to one another. It's called transactional analysis. You can find other books about it, and understanding how transactional analysis works in personal relationships will help you to change repetitive patterns in the way you interact with others.

Oh, and a few other things about relationships.

Be honest. When the sex is over, and I mean really over —both of you would prefer an early night and a thriller on Netflix, in separate rooms—it is time to talk.

If you are desperately fond of him but irritated to the screaming point by his habits (leaving the lid off the toothpaste and wet towels all over the bathroom floor), things have already gone too far. It's either talk, or nag. Nagging is not an option. The sooner you talk, the easier it will be. But if that doesn't work, make a decision. Can you face years of feeling sour and irritated? Or do you think that you can ignore the toothpaste and the towels?

This is a personal decision. If talking fails, then it's time to get pen and paper and write the way you feel about him in two columns: pluses and minuses.

Assess what works for you and what doesn't and stick to your priorities. Committing to action should be easier after that.

If you feel undervalued, by changing the pattern of transactions between you, you may restore the power balance.

35

YOU'RE NOT SANTA. SAY NO.

Would you hurt yourself to make
someone else happy? Don't. Boss Up.

I LOVE MY FAMILY, ESPECIALLY MY IMMEDIATE
family. I have an extended family too—cousins and aunties and so
on—who naturally can call on the resources of those who are best
off, which includes me.

If you don't have very much, and never have had very much, and
have never figured out how to save or invest, then somebody who's
richer than most people can seem super-rich, and somebody who's
truly super-rich can seem superhuman. So if you're just averagely
rich, as I am (as opposed to averagely poor) you can easily answer
too many requests with an automatic yes because—well, they're family. If you do, you'll create dependence and will end up resenting all
your relations. You can end up in the ridiculous situation where they
disrespect you for getting poorer, while the drain on your income
is them.

You have to respect your own worth. The worst thing you can do is hurt yourself to make someone else happy, whether or not that someone is related to you. You don't want him or her to feel bad or to think you don't care, but don't be a pushover. Talk to the person about the options and get something in writing. Signal any doubts if you have them, and learn to say no.

Here's how I learned—the hard way. A cousin called me. He wanted money to buy a bike and start a business. I asked him for more details, and he told me. He seemed to have thought it through. I knew that he'd never been a stand-out entrepreneur or worker, and he wasn't the sharpest knife in the box either, but I gave him the benefit of the doubt because he was family. I transferred some money to him.

About a day later I got a call. The cash had been stolen from him, and he was in hospital. He now needed (a) replacement money for the bike and (b) money for his hospital bill. He was so obviously confident that I'd give it to him that I was suspicious. I asked myself, *Had he paid for the bike and crashed it? Had he gambled what I'd sent?* I work so hard for my money, and I might not have it again. So I paid the hospital bill, but that was all.

He cursed me on the phone and sent me a threatening message about getting people to beat me up. Unbelievable.

I decided never to be a soft touch again. And since then I have refused to help dubious people like him, first cousin or not. He had manipulated my desire to do what I thought was right for my family and expected of me. I was trying to conform to an idea that I should look after the whole extended family.

Tough. I can't. I have to stand on my feet—and so does he.

Would you hurt yourself to make someone else happy? Don't. Boss Up.

36

BE YOUR OWN CHEERLEADER

It's your success.
Only you can make it.

'A PROPHET IS WITHOUT HONOUR ONLY IN HIS
home town, among his relatives, and in his own home,' Jesus said, no
doubt causing eyebrows to rise all over Nazareth.

We all want our families to cheer us on, and I'm lucky that mine
do. But sometimes you have to cheer for yourself. Familiarity breeds
a tendency to underestimate, and being a parent implies having the
last word until the child grows up.

I'd decided when I was in school that I'd be in films, and I
started studying for auditions when I was at university. My father
was appalled. Nothing a girl can say will change the mind of a parent who thinks his daughter's dream job will put her on a fast track
to social disaster, moral decline, and poverty, thereby wrecking the
future of the entire extended family, especially him.

I knew I had to take my destiny into my own hands, and that's what you have to do, too. Part of that is rejecting your parents' views. It's hard, but it's what growing up means: making your own mistakes, extricating yourself from problems on your own, and making your own success as well. It's sometimes lonely, but it's the truth—sometimes your parents won't be supportive. It's not their dream you're following, it's yours. Part of following your dream is accepting that and letting go of their expectations. They've got their own dreams (you hope). You have to fight for your own future. Boss Up! It's your success, and only you can make it.

It's your success. Only you can make it.

37

THE WORST MOMENT

*You never know how strong you are
until the situation presents itself.*

MY FATHER WAS ILL, OFF AND ON, FOR SIX OR
seven years. At one point, I flew him to India for treatment. I saw
him lying in his hospital bed, his head raised on pillows, with my
mother in a chair beside him. My father, who had always been so
strong, had covered his face with his hands. I lifted them gently.

'Don't cry, Daddy. Why are you crying?'

'I'm scared. I'm scared of my test results. Scared of so many
things.'

'Don't worry. You're here for treatment.'

We all prayed together, in awe, but powerless. He was in terrible
pain. Scared of dying. We knew that, so did he, but none of us said it.

I was there for two weeks and then came back to Nigeria. When
the phone rang, I'd whisper a prayer as I picked it up.

He was discharged, came home with my mother, began to recover... then he would relapse. One time he was really ill. The phone woke me at two in the morning. My mother was on the line, in despair.

'He's deteriorated so much,' she said. 'He can't talk, and he can't move.'

He was moved into a wheelchair and taken to hospital. I went to see him. He held my hand and whispered, 'I'm sorry, Chika.'

We both knew what he meant. It was nothing to do with being ill.

He couldn't say any more. He stayed there for ten days and then he was taken to a better-equipped hospital because he was too weak to move or swallow. He was sent straight to Intensive Care and hooked up to every kind of aid to life.

All of us prayed for him; my mother, my five siblings, and me. We were back and forth to the hospital. Around the middle of the following day, getting ready to go there again, I got another call from my mum.

'He's not responding to the treatment. They are trying to resuscitate him....' I heard talking in the background. Suddenly, 'I have to go,' she said.

She called back twenty minutes later. 'Your father has died, Chika.'

I burst into tears.

Within an hour, all his children had gathered at my brother's house. Together we went to the hospital and were taken into his room. The body had been prepared for removal to his village.

He looked so young. Mummy was holding him close and wailing and shaking. None of us knew what to do. I sat on the floor. I literally couldn't imagine my world without Daddy in it; it seemed to me that somehow if we all willed it, he would regain consciousness.

And then reality overwhelmed me. His death was real. I had known it would happen, of course I had—and yet I hadn't imagined this void, this terrifying sense of loss, of being alone. Grief reminded me how sad my poor father had been before he passed. I began to shake and cry and wail. I couldn't stop.

My sister consoled me. You never know how strong you are until the situation presents itself. In this situation, we had to be strong for my mother. Mommy was devastated. She kept saying, 'Is this it? Is this it?'

I said, 'God knows best.' But I was weeping, weeping.

Which was odd. Because I had loved my Daddy, and for most of my life, he'd hated me.

You never know how strong you are until the situation presents itself.

38

FORGIVE

'This thing'

A FEW YEARS AFTER THE DIVORCE, I WAS LIB-
erated from my marriage, self-reliant, and successful on my own. I
had been able to construct the life I wanted and lay the foundation
of better things to come.

My father had died. But I was still carrying the psychological
baggage that had weighed me down all my life. He had asked me for
forgiveness before he died. He had acknowledged his cruelty. But he
had been unable to explain why he had hated me when I was a child;
what 'this thing' was that made him see me as an outcast. All my life,
this secret thing had made me feel there was something wrong about
my whole identity.

I hoped to find out the truth now. I was in America at my
brother Felix's apartment. I'd come to see my mother. She wasn't well.

She'd been back and forth to stay with Felix several times since our father died.

Felix knew I intended to ask her why Daddy had been so unfair. I thought she'd probably be defensive and refuse to explain, as usual, so Felix would be a kind of mediator. That was the idea.

I don't know why, but something about being far from home made it easier for me to lay my cards on the table. So I did.

Mommy told me that it didn't matter anymore, to forget any hurt that there had been, and that God had been good to me. In short, she didn't give an inch. I loved her and respected her, but know what? There are limits.

Our relationship had always been loving and stormy at the same time. I'm an actress, she was a pastor, so there were some differences in our attitudes to life. I asked again, accusing her of holding back on the truth.

We had a two-hour screaming match. I screamed home truths. She screamed home truths. My brother was flapping around us looking aghast.

The neighbours—'Don't be so LOUD!' he pleaded 'This is America. The police will arrest you!'

It all ended with me slamming out, rushing to my bedroom, and flinging myself, sobbing, onto the bed like a teenager. I was doing the angry crying thing that I had learned to conquer in business, but this was a family issue, and frustration overwhelmed all control. I knew that she knew what I desperately needed to know, and for some reason she wouldn't say.

I was sitting, red-eyed, on the edge of the bed. I heard the door open. I looked up and then down. My mum had walked in. I was too angry to even talk to her.

She sat beside me and said in a low voice, 'I'm really sorry, Chika.'

That came as a shock. She had apologised before—she'd always taught us to apologise whenever we were wrong. But this was a different kind of apology.

'I'm really sorry. My dear girl.' She sat by me on the bed, held me, and hugged me tight while I wiped my eyes.

Then she moved to a chair, and said, 'I will tell you everything you need to know. I should not have kept this from you, but I want you to know I never meant to hurt you. I always wanted you to be strong and pull through. And you didn't disappoint me; I am proud of the woman you have become. But I am going to tell you what happened before you were born.'

I had seen photographs of her as a young woman. I'd stopped crying. I couldn't wait to hear what she would say. At the same time, I was full of fear. I might hear something that would change my life forever. But I was ready to hear the truth.

'Your father had told me when we married that he wanted to have only four children, including at least two boys. So we had a boy and two girls, and I got pregnant again. We were both happy, and Daddy knew that this one would have to be a boy, but we wanted to be sure, so we both went back to his village and we invited a soothsayer to come. He came to our compound to see us both. He gave us charms and chanted incantations. He laid his hands on my stomach and told me, 'You are pregnant. You are going to have a boy.'

Daddy was overjoyed. He sent people to get drinks for the soothsayer, and ordered two cows to be killed. He would throw a big feast so that the whole village could celebrate with us.

While food was being prepared he told this man, 'Now I want you to prove it. Prove to me that it's going to be a boy.'

The soothsayer had arrived carrying a long smooth stick. Now he stood up, took it in his hand and said, 'Do you see this wand? I'm going to throw it up in the air. If it falls to the ground, you will have a daughter. If it hangs, and floats in the air, you will have a son.'

He spoke an incantation and threw the wand high in the air.

And the wand stayed up. He didn't look at it. He kept talking to Daddy for over an hour and the wand was motionless, up in the air, just like magic. When it was time for him to leave, he held out his open hands, spoke an incantation, and the wand fell on his palm and he took it away.

Daddy was so happy. In the weeks afterwards, he started buying boy's clothes, boy's shoes, boy's everything. Everything in the house was blue, and whenever he went abroad he bought boy's things.

At one point, while your father was in Lagos, my cousin… you know, the pastor that you never met? He came to the village to see me. He prayed with me, and afterwards he told me I was going to have a girl. I burst into tears. I said, 'I don't want bad news like that. I am carrying a boy. It was confirmed by the soothsayer. Why are you trying to discourage me and make me feel bad? You know how much my husband wants a boy. Are you trying to spoil my mood?'

He said, 'No, I'm not trying to spoil your mood. I prayed, and God showed me that you're going to have a girl.'

So when Daddy came back from Lagos, I told him what my cousin said. He was furious. He said I must never, ever speak to him or let him into the house again.

I knew I had to remove the doubt in our minds, so I went to the hospital in Onitsha to have a scan. The doctor looked at the image and confirmed that the baby was a boy. I was so relieved. I went home, we celebrated. Your Daddy made such a fuss of me. He gave me everything I wanted because in his heart, I was carrying a boy.

The next time I went to that hospital I was in labour. The same doctor was there, the one who'd analysed the scan, so he was shocked when you came out and you were a girl. He said you must have changed in the womb. He told me, 'This is going to be a special child. I want to be her godfather.'

I'd never known before why a doctor we rarely saw was my godfather. ('Changed in the womb!' Anything rather than admit he'd made a mistake.) She went on.

'I wanted to feed you, but I couldn't. I was too scared when I thought of what your father would say. I just lay there crying. Daddy came to the hospital, saw you lying in your cot, and obviously you were a girl. He walked out and never came back. But I was still worried about what he would say when I took you home, and my milk would not flow at all. For the first few days the nurses had to bottle-feed you because you were yelling so much—you were a hungry baby. But they wanted me to be able to do it before I left, and they told me to stop crying. The milk came in, and I took you home.

'Chika, it wasn't easy. For four months he would not touch you or speak of you. He never lifted you up or carried you. It was as if he was trying to pretend you were not there. If he came into a room and saw you, he would walk out. This is when it started—with his disappointment. I was sad, and I asked my brothers to approach him. They changed his mind a little, he was softer after that, but he still hated you in his heart. He had wanted a boy so much. And when I did give birth to a boy I think he forgave me. But he never forgave you. I know you did not have an easy time.

'But that's how your name was given to you: Chikadibia, because it means 'God is greater than any soothsayer.''

Then, I finally understood. I forgave. And the psychological burden lifted.

Grief never leaves. It retreats into the background.

39

COPING WITH LOSS

Grief never leaves.
It retreats into the background.
You'll have to find ways to deal with it.

YOU KNOW YOUR PARENTS WON'T ALWAYS BE around, but there's a difference between knowing, in the abstract, and suddenly feeling the loss.

My mom was always a woman on the go, dashing from one person to another to help them, organising things—even after my father died. She called me one time when I was in Lagos. She said, 'I'm in the hospital. I fell and blacked out. The doctor says I need bed rest for two weeks!' Like it was the hardest thing anybody had ever been asked to do and life on earth would stop if she took two weeks off.

But she had been warned. I had told her, and her doctor had told her, that if she kept going like a runaway train, she'd crash.

After Dad died, I relied on her kindness and gentle goodness more than ever. Not that we were always in the same house, or city, or even the same country. Nor that we didn't occasionally have stand-up rows about stupid things. I wasn't a child any more, and sometimes I thought she forgot that. All the same, we only ever had one really shouty, resentful, bitter confrontation, when I demanded to know the truth of my father's hatred for me. Then we apologised and hugged and made up. We were both in America, but I was flying home to Lagos the next day. She'd stay on in Utah with my brother.

Three months later he told me she wasn't at all well. A lesion on her back just wouldn't heal. My youngest sister was in America too, and pregnant, and she advised him to get Mummy's sugar levels tested. My sister was right. Mum had Type 2 diabetes. Her blood sugar was sky high. She took the right medication, but I don't think she got advice about diet and exercise. Her diabetes was already far advanced.

She was dozy most of the time. She called me and asked me to get her a ticket home. I said, 'That's crazy! You're in the best place! America is where you should be for health care.'

'No,' she said. 'These Americans... they don't know how to treat black people.'

'Find a black doctor then. Anyway, there are thousands of black diabetics in America, they get treatment. No. I'm not getting you a ticket. The care here is not nearly as good as you can get over there.'

We kept in touch, mostly through my brother. She didn't seem to be improving much. Then I got a call from my pastor.

'Chika, now I don't want you to be angry.'

'What? What's the matter?'

'Your mother is home. She's here, in Lagos.'

'How? What happened?'

'Nothing. She's okay. She told me not to tell you she was coming.'

'Why? What's wrong?'

'She wants to see her own doctor here. About her diabetes.'

'That's just silly, self-defeating…. She makes me so angry. She won't be helped.'

'Calm down. Calm down, Chika. She would like to see you.'

She was staying with my youngest sister, who had come back after having her baby. Mum was so frail and thin. She had aged dramatically in about a month and could hardly walk. It was terrible. I hugged her, and tears came to my eyes.

'What happened to you, Mummy?'

'I don't know. I just feel so ill. I have back pain, I have diabetes, I ache all over.'

Slowly, she faded. There was no drama; just a life full of pills and doctors and hospitals, and struggling along in poor health, which worsened for a long, miserable time until one day, she was gone. Such a good person, who had helped so many people, who had been assertive and confident, and yet illness had left her without the confidence or the will to help herself. I just couldn't reconcile myself to her death. I wept at the funeral, as we all did. I grieved. But I didn't get over it. She had left a huge vacancy in my life. For months I had panic attacks, and for a while I lost the power of speech. I was not coping well.

There were six of us. With both our parents gone, what would hold us together? We all had different jobs, different interests. We didn't attend the same church or live in the same part of town. We even grieved separately. That was hard. It seemed the string that bound us together had vanished.

Somehow good came out of bad, as it usually does. Whenever we get together, and we still do, we remember my mum. As the acute pain of her death has lessened, I rejoice more and more in the life she led.

Her greatest quality was generosity of spirit. I sometimes ask myself, 'What would Mum have done?' and a brisk, kind, practical answer always comes to me.

Grief never leaves. It retreats into the background. You'll have to find ways to deal with it.

BOSS UP! TO DO LIST

Do you have a family member who needs your forgiveness? Why haven't you forgiven?

Can you take baby steps to reaching out and forgiving that person?

Do you have an active family chat group?

Do you call your parents to tell them you love them (they won't be here forever, do it often)?

Are you emotionally dependent on someone and have they tried to control you emotionally? What can you do to get your emotional independence back?

If your plans diverged (for instance, if your partner wanted to work in one city, and you in another), could you negotiate a compromise that suited both of you perfectly well?

Do you feel you can't do what you want unless you have a partner? If so, why?

Write a letter to someone you love (could be your mum, dad, boyfriend, girlfriend, wife, or husband). Tell this person how grateful you are to have her (or him) and encourage all the good behaviors you love about her (or him).

PART 6

GRACE

'Let us have confidence, then, and approach God's throne, where there is grace. There we will receive mercy and find grace to help us just when we need it.'

—Hebrews 4:16

40

STAY GRATEFUL

'A grateful heart is a
magnet for miracles.'

WHEN PEOPLE GIVE YOU THINGS OR DO THINGS for you, be grateful. Be grateful for everything; trees, sunshine, your lover, the sand on the beach, your life, your senses, your abilities, your family, your dog, and your cat. Look around you and be happy.

An ungrateful state of mind is negative. If you're not grateful for the beauty of a tree or a river or mobility, you might as well not exist. Gratitude makes you happy. Greedy people are never happy because they are never satisfied with what they have—only ungrateful. Non-believers can be just as happy and grateful as those who have a God, it's just that they don't have anything to be grateful to. I know... weird.

There is a saying: 'If you thank a king for the good he has done, he will give you more.'

I originally learned this the other way round: if you don't thank a king properly he'll take away what you already have. My father, noticing how tall I already was at the age of nine, gave me a new bicycle because my old one was too small for me. I was thrilled. I pedalled down the road on it. Another little girl had a new bike too, and she'd left it outside her house. It was pink, and it had a basket on the front and a pump.

'So, do you like your new bicycle?' my father asked me when I came back.

I told him yes. I also told him that I'd just seen my friend's new bike and it was pink and it had a basket.

He looked at me oddly.

'Are you saying you want me to change your bike for one like hers?'

'Yes, please,' I said eagerly. 'Oh, yes, please!'

The next day I couldn't find my bike. Not my new bike. Not any bike. So I asked Daddy.

'Daddy, where is my bike? I can't find it!'

'I gave it to one of the kids down the street. He's never had a bike at all, and his whole face lit up when I gave it to him.'

He had taught me a valuable lesson. I was privileged. I'm older now, and I see how many girls are ungrateful. Complaining on Facebook about their 'rubbish old phones' and telling the world their father's 'too mean' to buy them a new one. That sort of thing.

When you get older, you notice how many children don't even have parents to love them or care at all for them or even about them. And how many couples desperately want children but can't have them. Love is fundamental to all of us, and yet some of us don't have anyone to give it to or receive it from. Of course, the material things are important too—shelter, clean water, and food, for a start.

But a bicycle? Certainly high on the list if it's your only quick way of getting to school. But that didn't excuse me for offending my father.

Please see your disappointments in proportion to your blessings, and value your gifts every day. And remember that everything we have is a gift.

'A grateful heart is a magnet for miracles.'

41

THE MASTER KEY

'Is prayer your steering wheel
or your spare tire?'

Corrie ten Boom

IN BIBLE STUDIES AT SCHOOL WE USED TO SING:

Prayer is the key
Prayer is the key
Prayer is the master key;
Jesus started with prayer
And ended with prayer
Prayer is the master key.

In my life, that has been true. People ask why I attach so much importance to religion. How could I not? I grew up in the church. My mum was a pastor, and we knew her friends and colleagues who were pastors, choristers, evangelists, and bishops. So I was always a churchgoer. I know the value of kneeling humbly to ask for some-thing. At my worst points I pray, and my prayer is usually answered.

Most of us need a spiritual belief to hold onto—a higher power to talk to and worship. I am a Christian, so I pray to the God in my mind, and if you are a Muslim you do the same thing. It is so peaceful when you pray.

I believe that God sees into everyone's heart, and in times of pain and bitterness and grief He will help us. After my mother died, when I was panicking and I couldn't speak, I couldn't even think properly. I found it really hard to come to terms with her death, but I asked God for direction and He was there for me.

I know that people may not be there when I need them, but God will always be there for me. He listens and acts. He makes no promises except for His presence and love in my life. He is my Father, and I can confide in Him.

My story is told only by the grace of God, which has given me good fortune far beyond anything I could have hoped for.

BOSS UP! TO DO LIST

Do you talk to God everyday?

How often do you pause to appreciate the things
you have?

List 10 things you are grateful for (it could be anything,
the trees, your children, your job)

Do you meditate everyday at least for 10 minutes?

Before you fall asleep reflect on 5 things you are grateful
for daily .

Do you think you have an attitude of gratitude?

Start practicing gratitude .

Conclusion

Congratulations!!! Drum roll... roll out the red carpet... lights and camera clicks. The spotlight is on you.

I am certain that there isn't anything you can't achieve or conquer. You have BOSSED UP! Go out there and kick ass! Nothing should hold you back—not even you!

I'm so proud of you for finishing this book. I know it's not easy to take the time to read in this fast-paced world of social media distractions, but you did it for you, and I am super proud of the new level you've attained by completing this book.

I hope you've learnt something from this book that will be a useful tool in your life. I hope by sharing my lessons, I can help you achieve your goals and live your best life.

You can achieve whatever you want to achieve. Believe in yourself, love yourself, trust your intuition, and never stop trying. Never, never, never give up!

Remember, I'm rooting for you, and I want to see you live your best life.

Please drop me a note or comment through my website or social media pages:

> www.chikaike.com
> Instagram: Chikaike
> Facebook: Chikaike
> Twitter: Chikaike

Can't wait to hear from you!
Love you.

Acknowledgments

I want to say thanks to God Almighty who created me and gave me this magnificent, beautiful, and wonderful life filled with blessings, divine favour, and grace. Sometimes I feel undeserving of all my blessings and humbled at how far I've come from that little girl with a dream.

I'm certain God has read this book and approved of all the chapters and words. Thank you, God, for giving me all I needed and allowing me to go through all these experiences and become a stronger person. And most importantly, thank you for giving me the mind-set to BOSS UP!

Thanks to my late mum, who I know is watching over me, for all she sacrificed for me, all the encouragement and love she showered on me. She believed I could when everyone doubted. I wish you were here to read this book. You told me I needed to write a book and share my experiences with the world. I've done it, and I'm sure it will make you proud. Thanks to my late Dad, who is my superhero. He built me to face the world and all its challenges. Thanks for all the love and support you showed me.

Thanks to my siblings, Chuks, Nkiru, Chinyere, Kenechi, and Chubby. You've been my greatest cheerleaders and have loved me unconditionally. Thanks to my sister-in-laws, brother-in-laws, and my beautiful nieces and nephew. You always bring out the child in me and teach me never to take life too serious.

Thanks to my close friend and publicist Serah for your constant support and encouragement. And being on this roller coaster ride with me. Thanks for being my rock during some of the toughest periods of my life and giving me a shoulder to cry on.

Thanks to all my friends who have played one role or the other in my life.

Thanks to all my colleagues who have inspired me to be a better person and work harder at achieving my goals.

Thanks to my amazing team home and far away, for your help in making all my set goals come true and for working endlessly on other projects. I know I can sometimes be a handful and overly passionate about deadlines. Thank you for waking you at odd hours to discuss a new idea or project with me.

Thanks to all my mentors who have advised and mentored me all through the years. Thanks to my personal coach, Dafna, my HBS living group members, PLD25, and all the professors and administrative team of the Harvard Business School who have transformed me in ways words can't express.

Thanks to my late dog Reese. You were the best gift for 12 years of my life.

Thanks to all the strong women around the world who set the pace and constantly motivate and inspire me.

Thanks to Oprah for being my role model and for providing me with a wonderful model—someone I have looked up to and has never disappointed me.

A huge thank you to my social media friends, fans, and lovers. You are awesome.

Love you.